T0301827

Cities and the Urban Land Premium

Cities and the Urban Land Premium

Henri L.F. de Groot

VU University Amsterdam, Tinbergen Institute and Ecorys NEI, the Netherlands

Gerard Marlet

Atlas voor Gemeenten, Utrecht University School of Economics and University of Groningen, the Netherlands

Coen Teulings

University of Cambridge, UK, University of Amsterdam and Tinbergen Institute, the Netherlands

Wouter Vermeulen

CPB Netherlands Bureau for Economic Policy Analysis, the Netherlands

Edward Elgar
PUBLISHING

Cheltenham, UK • Northampton, MA, USA

Published by
Edward Elgar Publishing Limited
The Lypiatts
15 Lansdown Road
Cheltenham
Glos GL50 2JA
UK

Edward Elgar Publishing, Inc.
William Pratt House
9 Dewey Court
Northampton
Massachusetts 01060
USA

A catalogue record for this book
is available from the British Library

Library of Congress Control Number: 2014959498

This book is available electronically in the **Elgar**online
Economics subject collection
DOI 10.4337/9781784717445

ISBN 978 1 78471 743 8 (cased)
ISBN 978 1 78471 744 5 (eBook)

Typeset by Servis Filmsetting Ltd, Stockport, Cheshire
Printed and bound in Great Britain by CPI Group (UK Ltd)

Contents

Preface

After a long period of suburbanisation, since the 1980s cities have been in vogue again. But why? Why are people prepared to spend far more money on a small house in the city than on a large house in the countryside – and why doesn't this apply to all cities?

The appeal of the city in the twenty-first century is not only determined by the production side of the economy, but also by the consumption side: its array of shops, cultural activities and, for instance, a historic city centre. All these factors translate into land prices that are worlds apart and also, where production is concerned, into different wages for urban and rural citizens. This study maps out all these differences. The fact that land prices reflect the appreciation for those urban amenities makes them an essential measurement tool in the cost–benefit analyses for local investments and spatial planning policies and this sheds a new light on the organisation of public administration.

This book is meant to be an accessible read for a wide audience. We have avoided complex mathematical and econometric calculations. For the purpose of readability, references to literature have also been limited. This kind of background information is available to the interested reader on the website that accompanies this study (www.cpb.nl/stadenland).

This book is the result of an intensive collaboration between the researchers of the CPB Netherlands Bureau for Economic Policy Analysis, *Atlas voor Gemeenten* (the Municipal Atlas) and VU University Amsterdam. CPB has been taking a more intensive look at the meaning of location for economic activity for several years now. In its 2010 study 'The Netherlands of 2040', cities take a prominent place. This present book puts flesh on the bones of that analysis, both in empirical and policy terms. In its publication *The Attractive City* (*De Aantrekkelijke Stad*) in 2009, *Atlas voor Gemeenten* documented the correlation between house prices and numerous local amenities. We also build on that in this book. Chapters 4 and 8 draw from scientific journal papers published in the *Journal of Regional Science* (Groot, De Groot and Smit, 2015, Regional Wage Differences in the Netherlands) and the *Journal of Benefit–Cost Analysis* (Vermeer and Vermeulen, 2012, External Benefits of Brownfield Redevelopment). The main conclusions from this book have been summarised in the box at the end of this preface.

CBS Statistics Netherlands (*Centraal Bureau voor de Statistiek*) and the NVM Dutch Association of Real Estate Brokers (*Nederlandse Vereniging van Makelaars*) made an important contribution to this study through the disclosure of data.

Frits Bos, Stefan Groot, Martijn Smit, Niels Vermeer, Clemens van Woerkens and Annette Zeilstra collaborated on various chapters. Jasper Dekkers and Friso de Vor rendered technical support in accessing the NVM data. John Blokdijk and Jelte Haagsma created the illustrative figures. George Gelauff, Harry Garretsen, Fré Huizinga, Ruud Okker, Ioulia Ossokina, Maarten 't Riet, Eugène Verkade and Bas ter Weel commented on the texts. Secretarial support throughout this study was provided by Jannie Droog.

THE FIVE MOST IMPORTANT CONCLUSIONS FROM THIS STUDY

The price of land in the Amsterdam city centre is 200 times as high as that in the countryside of East-Groningen. This price difference more than doubled between 1985 and 2007. The importance of location has, therefore, grown considerably.

The wage surplus of agglomeration and urbanisation ranges between 3 and 10 billion euro, or 0.5% and 2% of the GDP. The total differential land value boils down to approximately 340 billion euro (excluding land for commercial purposes), which corresponds to an annual return of 15 billion euro, or 3% of the GDP.

77% of the land price differences can be explained by a limited number of factors, such as access to jobs, nuisance and amenities such as culture, shops and restaurants and cafes. Factors on the production side of the economy (access to jobs) and consumer amenities each explain approximately 50% of the land price differences. The presence of luxury shops, a historical city centre, bars and restaurants and cultural amenities together determine 30% of the land price differences.

The best way to finance a municipality is through a tax on the land value surplus. The increase in the Netherlands in the General Grant from the Municipal Fund (*Algemene Uitkering uit het Gemeentefonds*) per resident, according to the size of the population, is a second best alternative to a tax on the land value.

Since land price differentials reflect the user benefit of local public facilities, they are an excellent basis for social cost–benefit analyses and the best tax base for funding local governments.

Henri de Groot, Gerard Marlet, Coen Teulings
and Wouter Vermeulen

1. The resurrection of the city

> Great cities are not like towns, only larger. They are not like
> suburbs, only denser.
> Jane Jacobs, 1961

Cities are as old as the road to Jericho. People tend to go where others
are. That is where they can benefit from the merchandise that others have
to offer and from the many opportunities to build a network, find jobs,
exchange knowledge and ideas or seek a marriage partner. The geographical space is, therefore, not neutral. Activity concentrates in certain locations creating spiky economic landscapes. Due to the concentration of
activity, those locations are appealing and the land is expensive. The price
of land is the best measure of the attractiveness of such locations, and
hence for the excess value of urbanisation.

   The concentration of people in a certain location makes cities one of
the most important targets for politics and public policy. After all, there
are external effects: the well-being of city dwellers is inextricably linked
to their neighbours' presence and activities. Therefore, they must mutually agree. That requires a complex form of political decision making.
The advantages of urbanisation in both a material and immaterial sense
are great. But how can these advantages be achieved? Furthermore, does
everyone benefit equally greatly from the advantages, or are there winners
and losers? In case of the latter, is there any compensation? These questions make urbanisation a key point of departure for economic policy, and
they turn the measure of that urbanisation – land prices – into key policy
information. For that reason, this study aims to provide more insight into
the importance of urbanisation and the way in which the advantages can
be utilised to the maximum through economic policy.

THE FIRST WAVE: THE NEOLITHIC REVOLUTION

Cities emerged as a by-product of agricultural development during the
Neolithic revolution, around 10000 years ago. Around that time, agri-
culture started to gradually develop in what we now call the Middle East.
Hunting and gathering, the traditional means of existence, gave way to

active agriculture. Paul Bairoch gave a beautiful description of the rich history of urban development (see further reading). Independent of each other, Neolithic revolutions took place in multiple places around the world, beginning in the Middle East, then the Americas, Europe, and Asia and eventually reaching Africa. The Neolithic revolution was thus not a coincidence. Again and again, cities emerged shortly after the first stage of the revolution. Jericho is considered to be the oldest city. In a traditional society of exclusively hunters and gatherers, the density of the population in even the most fertile areas could not rise above a few persons per square kilometre. Agriculture enabled the density of the population to increase by no less than a factor of one hundred. This allowed for a small surplus in food production that could be transported to a central place, a city, where people could busy themselves with other activities. In a traditional society with its low density of population, the distances over which the food must be transported were simply too great. In an economic sense, the rise in population density is, therefore, equivalent to the decline in the food transportation cost. The proximity of others in the city allowed for specialisation, so that people could afford a more varied consumption pattern through mutual exchange. Cities were inevitably a marketplace to facilitate that exchange. Due to the high transportation costs, it was simply impossible in traditional societies to benefit from the advantages of specialisation. This is a recurrent topic in the history of urbanisation. It turns out that the declining importance of transportation costs actually makes it attractive to people to gather in one place. The world does not become flatter. On the contrary, more peaks emerge where economic prosperity clusters.

The city also offered another advantage. Violence is inherent in Neolithic societies. Azar Gat described how one in four people in Neolithic societies were killed by violence (see further reading). The advantage of the city was the relative safety offered by its high city walls. It was behind those walls that precarious specialisations such as goldsmiths could thrive that would be unimaginable without that protection against robbery and theft. Clive Ponting (see further reading) mentioned a second advantage of the walled town: it provided a clear demarcation of the urban area, and thereby also of the applicability of urban rules and legislation. That way, and with the help of a limited number of city gates, the city council could control trade and levy taxes.

The possibility of concentrating safety and surpluses in one place did, however, also create new opportunities for the gathering of larger groups in the shape of 'gangs of robbers' or 'armies'. These could be used for coordinated robbery or theft. The city – with its concentration of prosperity and economic activity – was a tempting magnet for these types of thievery. The pattern that has repeated itself throughout history, made its first entry. The risk of robbery opened up a market for protection. The distinction between robber and protector is, however, extremely subtle, as the mafia, in cities such as Naples, still demonstrates on a daily basis.

His status as lord protector gave the absolute sovereign the legitimacy for – often relentless – taxation. Those who did not want to submit to this protection – that is to say, those who did not want to pay taxes – fell prey to the unpleasant characteristics of the protector. The rise of the city thus went hand in hand with an explosion of income inequality. The ups and downs of the cities in that period were, therefore, more related to the magnitude of the tax base of the relevant sovereign than to the surplus value of specialisation and the marketplace that enabled it. Successful cities in that period were first and foremost key centres of prosperous kingdoms.

THE SECOND WAVE: TRANSATLANTIC TRADE AND INDUSTRIALISATION

For a long period, however, agriculture remained a labour-intensive activity. The percentage of people who lived in cities therefore remained limited to approximately 10 per cent of the population. In successful regions, that percentage could be slightly higher. Table 1.1 shows the development of the urbanisation rate in a number of European countries since 1300. Around that time, the urbanisation rate in the then prosperous countries of Europe – Spain and Italy – was around 15 to 20 per cent. The only exception was the current Belgium, where the urbanisation rate was already around 30 per cent. During the following centuries little changed, except in the Low Countries. Urbanisation in Belgium continued to increase, but the development in the Netherlands was even more extreme. Around 1700, the urbanisation rate in the Netherlands was considerably above the rest of Europe, and it remained that way until well into the 1800s. Jan de Vries and Ad van der Woude referred to this period in the Netherlands as the first round of modern economic growth. The Netherlands can, therefore, be rightfully called the birthplace of modern urbanisation. What happened in Dutch cities in the sixteenth and seventeenth centuries was the preface to the Industrial Revolution. As soon as that revolution slowed, first in the current Belgium and during the eighteenth century also in the current Netherlands, urbanisation also came to a halt. In the course of the nineteenth century, the Netherlands surrendered its first place on the urbanisation ladder to the rapidly and successfully industrialising England. In the following period, the urbanisation rate in the Netherlands rose again – when the Industrial Revolution also unfolded there; the arrival of railways added a little extra. Like elsewhere,

Table 1.1   Urbanisation rate of European countries (1300–1980)

Country	1300	1500	1700	1800	1910	1980
Belgium	25–35	30–45	26–35	18–22	57	70
England	6–9	7–9	13–16	22–24	75	79
France	9–11	9–12	11–15	11–13	38	69
Germany	5–8	7–9	8–11	8–10	49	75
Italy	15–21	15–20	14–19	16–20	(40)	65
Netherlands	8–12	20–26	38–49	34–39	53	82
Portugal	8–11	11–13	18–23	14–17	16	34
Russia	3–6	3–6	4–7	5–7	(14)	61
Spain	13–18	10–16	12–17	12–19	(38)	73
Switzerland	5–7	6–8	6–8	6–8	33	58
Europe	7–9	7–9	9–12	9–11	41	66

Notes:
The urbanisation rate is defined as a percentage of the population that resides in municipalities with a population greater than 5000. The borders of the countries are based on the situation in 1913.

Source: Paul Bairoch, *Cities and Economic Development: From the Dawn of History to the Present.*

railway construction in the Netherlands halfway through the nineteenth century brought a revolutionary reduction in travel times. The travel times between the most important cities of Holland, compared to those achieved on the famous canal boats were, on average, reduced by a factor of five. Since at first it was mainly the cities that were connected through the railway network, it heightened the urbanisation trend. Cities became more than a match for the countryside. Today, urbanisation rates of 70 per cent or more are not unusual. In other words, urbanisation and the rapid economic growth after the Industrial Revolution are inextricably linked.

A key factor in the acceleration of economic growth in Europe was the intercontinental sea trade that expanded enormously after the discovery of America by Europeans and the sea route around the Cape of Good Hope. But why did Spain and Portugal, which were both at the origins of this trade, only benefit from it for a very short time? After a peak around 1700, the urbanisation rate in Portugal declined again strongly in the course of the eighteenth century. In that same period, urbanisation in the Netherlands, and later in England, continued at full speed. John Bradford DeLong and Andrei Shleifer (see further reading) as well as Daron Acemoglu, Simon Johnson, and James Robinson demonstrated (see further reading) that it was more difficult for countries with an absolute monarch to profit from the new opportunities offered by the sea trade than for countries where power was more widely distributed. Absolute monarchy kills entrepreneurship, as the monarch stifles every business initiative with high taxes for their pride and splendour. Madrid and Lisbon remained royal residences, where stolen gold from America was spent on palaces like the Escorial. The Netherlands had its Great Revolt and England its Glorious Revolution, which curtailed the power of the king and thereby created the conditions for later growth. That brought an end to the era of successful royal residences.

THE THIRD WAVE: URBAN TRANSFORMATION AND THE CONSUMER CITY

However strong the connection is between urbanisation and economic growth, this link does not mean that every individual city in highly developed countries always flourishes. Philippe Oswalt's *Atlas of Shrinking Cities* (see further reading) provides an overview of cities that have shrunk significantly over the course of time. Table 1.2 includes some examples of cities in highly developed countries that underwent a period of decline in the course of the last century; it is more the rule than the exception and numerous successful metropolises are listed. The Dutch cities of Amsterdam and Rotterdam knew a period of decline; both lost more than 20 per cent of their population between 1960 and 1980. The emergence of

Table 1.2   Periods of decline in a number of major cities

City	Starting year	Final year	Decline (in %)
Amsterdam	1960	1988	21
Barcelona	1981	2000	15
Boston	1950	1980	30
London	1938	1991	23
Milan	1970	2001	31
Munich	1971	2000	9
New York	1970	1980	10
Paris	1954	1999	25
Rotterdam	1960	1988	21
San Francisco	1950	1980	12
Tokyo	1965	1999	11

Source: Philip Oswalt, *Atlas of Shrinking Cities.*

the squatter movement in Amsterdam was, therefore, not a reflection of an increase in left-wing activism or speculation by property owners, but rather a logical consequence of the enormous lack of occupancy resulting from the decreasing need for home and business properties. At that same time, the famous Times Square in New York mainly housed sex shops. Better tenants could simply not be found. Around 1980, when this phenomenon of decline was at its height, it became quite fashionable to speak of the 'death of the city'.

This obituary was a bit premature; after the mid 1980s, a great number of cities in highly developed countries were on the rise again. Although the communication and transportation costs were rapidly declining, a number of cities seemed to be recovering from the decline. They developed into appealing living environments, in which new ideas could sprout. Inner cities were turned into centres of entertainment, a process that Americans also refer to as the 'disneyfication' of the city. It was the time in which old docks were transformed into luxury residential areas, with fascinating examples such as Liverpool and Hamburg. Living at the waterfront became 'the thing to do'. Property prices rose. Populations grew again.

According to urban sociologists it was during this time of increasing globalisation that many people started to feel the need for the authenticity of the amenities in a (historic) city centre. Aesthetics and cultural and culinary experiences in those city centres turned out to be irreproducible on the Internet – a mistake that many made in the 1980s. A great number of goods could now be purchased over a distance, but not the perceptions and experiences that a city centre had to offer. That is the paradox of urban triumph. The development of the CD made it possible to bring a concert with perfect sound quality into your own living room. Nevertheless, the concerts of top artists sold out quicker than ever before. Digital sports channels allowed you to follow each game from beginning to end from your armchair, with a beer in your hand. Nevertheless, the crowds in the football stadiums were larger than ever. The need for new experiences, the urge to be there and feel it, the increased leisure time, the higher incomes and the greater work and care pressures all contributed to the desire of many consumers to have urban amenities as close to their homes as possible. It allowed them to spontaneously consume those amenities at any moment of every day. It allowed them to combine hard work with a large amount of relaxation. And this required *walking cities*: cities that have a great variety of urban amenities to offer at walking or cycling distance from home. The emergence of the consumer city explains in part the recovery of the city.

That recovery, however, is not typical of all cities. Take a trip to Detroit, for instance. The once flourishing city of Ford and General Motors continues to lose ground. Closer to home, the Dutch cities of Heerlen and Sittard have not been able to recuperate from the closure of the coal mines. Cities in the Randstad, the urban agglomeration of western Holland, are not immune to decline either. Rotterdam has not recovered from the crumbling of employment in its seaport, and the level of income there is one of the lowest in the Netherlands. The populations of Vlaardingen and Spijkenisse have been on the decline over recent years and even Almere, a newly planned town from the 1970s, has a reasonable chance of shrinkage in population in the not-so-faraway future. The pressing question is, therefore, why one city recovers, while another merely continues to be ailing. Why did Boston and Amsterdam manage to do what Detroit and Rotterdam could not? Edward Glaeser (see further reading) argued that the all-determining factor is the presence of universities: a permanent influx of higher-educated people enables a city to revive itself. When the ports of Boston were forced to close down during the 1970s and 80s, the flood of alumni from Harvard and MIT spawned the emergence of new activities: IT, investment banking and biomedical research. Now, Boston is flourishing as never before. Likewise, Amsterdam has had greater success than Rotterdam in holding on to its alumni and attracting the highly educated from elsewhere. It is thus the interplay of the appeal as a consumer city and the capability of putting oneself on the map as a production city that are decisive for urban success. Especially the most talented people, who are able to develop new production activities, need the varied cultural amenities that are typical of the consumer city. It is especially the higher educated who greatly benefit from living in the modern, attractive cities. They are, not surprisingly, prepared to pay more for a dwelling in the city. Consequently, on average there are more city dwellers among them than any other group – which raises numerous pressing policy questions about segregation and social cohesion.

The current blossoming of the city and the emergence of the knowledge economy are thus closely knit. Especially when it comes to innovation, the physical distance is still a decisive bottleneck. Coincidental meetings – a good talk near the coffee machine – are key ingredients for the development of new ideas. In itself, that phenomenon goes much further back than the 1980s. Klaus Desmet and Esteban Rossi-Hansberg (see further reading) showed how in the first decades of the last century, industry gradually moved to large cities. The invention of the electromotor and, more generally, the availability of electricity enabled a complete reorganisation of manufacturing processes. Electricity is a general purpose technology, an innovation that enabled a revolution in the entire production process and the city offered the ideal environment in which to benefit from that development. Once this innovation wave had died down, the city was no longer

the right environment for industry. Industry is a land-intensive activity and
the high land prices made the city an unattractive location. In the 1950s,
a gradual de-industrialisation process began: Table 1.2 clearly shows
its consequences for the urban population. In the 1980s, a new general
purpose technology made its entrance: information technology. This
technology caused a revolution, especially in the service industry. Again,
the city proved to be the ideal environment to utilise these new opportunities. Instead of manufacturing industry, it is now the service industry that
moves to the city. More than during the Industrial Revolution, information technology makes a strong appeal to the higher educated, causing a
strong migration to the city especially of this group – with consequences
for the composition of the population, both between and within cities.

This short sketch of history shows that the growth of a city is not self-
evident. Cities grow and decline, depending on the success of their specialisation. The once very successful textile industry in the Dutch cities of
Tilburg, Helmond and Enschede was moved to Asia some decades later.
The textile cities were in danger of being swept away in its fall. When the
fine days of the car industry in the United States were over, Detroit was
hit hard. After the fall of Lehman, London and New York were suffering.
On a macroeconomic level, it turns out that there is a pattern in the growth
and decline of cities. The rule of thumb is that the results achieved in the
past offer no guarantees for the future. It is partly a matter of coincidental
growth and decline, which contributes to a very specific distribution in the
magnitude of cities, known as Zipf's Law.

THE IMPORTANCE OF LAND PRICES

The great importance of clustering similar activities in one location (also
referred to as agglomeration) has the effect that the activities performed
by the one specific location exert great influence on the appeal of that location as a place of business or residence to others; that is how cities emerge.
The land prices in urban locations are, therefore, higher than those in
rural areas. In turn, these high land prices lead to a selection process. The
activities that have little to win by agglomeration with others go and look
for a cheaper place. The spot that becomes available is filled by exactly
those who stand to gain more than averagely from it. Through productivity effects that correlate with clustering, the wages in cities are also higher
than in rural areas. Again, a circular process arises through which workers
and businesses move to the city.

This way, a specialisation pattern comes about with the specific structure of a city, often with a Central Business District (CBD) and an extensive layout of residential neighbourhoods and suburbs surrounding it. But a specialisation pattern between the city and the countryside also emerges, in which industrial activities for which proximity is relatively unimportant congregate in the more peripheral areas, and services concentrate in the densely populated urban areas. A need arises for a transport infrastructure, to transport people from home to work. That infrastructure in itself leads to new differences in land prices, and thereby to further spatial specialisation. Land prices thus reflect the quality of the environment, and wages are partly the reflection of the productivity effects that go together with agglomeration. Since land prices reflect the quality of the environment – the public amenities and the concentration of knowledge and jobs – they are an ideal point of departure for the valuation of investments in it. The effect of the development of a public facility on the land prices in its direct surroundings is an adequate measure for its added social value. Land prices are, therefore, an important input for social cost–benefit analyses (SCBAs). That is why spatial differences in land prices and wages are central to this book.

Hidden behind the impact of the proximity of amenities on land prices and wages lies a deeper question: how can this process of spatial specialisation and city formation be best organised? Can we let nature take its course, and do cities then grow by themselves, or do we need some form of spatial planning? What are the consequences for social cohesion? City formation is clearly accompanied by major external effects: the choice of location by the one has great consequences for the value of other locations. That fact in itself already suggests that political intervention is needed. But how can that intervention best be designed?

THE FIVE MOST IMPORTANT CONCLUSIONS

Industrialisation caused the degree of urbanisation to jump from 20% to 70%; that step was first taken in the Netherlands in the seventeenth century.

The success of cities is not self-evident. Cities grow and decline according to a pattern that is difficult to predict.

The modern city is inextricably linked to the knowledge economy, as the exchange of new ideas runs quicker face-to-face.

During the last decade, the variety in consumption possibilities developed into an important added value for the city.

Land prices reflect the value of public facilities and are, therefore, an important input for social cost–benefit analyses (SCBAs).

FURTHER READING

Daron Acemoglu, Simon Johnson and James Robinson, 2005, The rise of Europe: Atlantic trade, institutional change, and economic growth, *American Economic Review*, 95(3), 546–79.

Paul Bairoch, 1988, *Cities and Economic Development: From the Dawn of History to the Present*, University of Chicago Press, Chicago.

James Bradford DeLong and Andrei Shleifer, 1993, Princes and merchants: City growth before the Industrial Revolution, *Journal of Law and Economics*, 36, 671–702.

Klaus Desmet and Esteban Rossi-Hansberg, 2008, Spatial growth and industry age, *Journal of Economic Theory*, 144, 2477–502.

Azar Gat, 2006, *War in Human Civilization*, Oxford University Press, Oxford.

Edward Glaeser, 2005, Reinventing Boston: 1640–2003, *Journal of Economic Geography*, 5(2), 119–53.

Philippe Oswalt, 2006, *Atlas of Shrinking Cities*, Hatje Cantz Verlag, Germany.

Clive Ponting, 1991, *A Green History of the World: The Environment and the Collapse of Great Civilizations*, Penguin Books, New York.

2.   Land underneath the city

Corn is not high because rents are high, but rents are high
because corn is high.
David Ricardo, 1817

Where harvests are plentiful, agricultural land is expensive. Where people like to live, the land underneath their homes has great value. It is not the land prices that dictate those for homes, but it is the popularity of the dwelling and its location that determine the land price. Contrary to what policy makers often believe, high land and house prices are not an indication of a city in trouble, but rather that it is doing very well. Dutch cities are indeed doing very well. But things have been different.

In the 1960s and 1970s, a suburbanisation wave hit the Netherlands; the countryside was winning ground over the city. As increasingly more people could afford a car, increasingly more people could afford to live in a larger home in a green environment at a greater distance from their work in the city. Moreover, employment in, for example, the shipyards in northern Amsterdam was also rapidly declining. The major cities in the Netherlands, such as Amsterdam, lost perhaps a quarter of their population at this time (Figure 2.1).

No wonder that, thirty years ago, many thought that cities were threatened and that everybody would eventually like to live in a safe, green environment. What would be left were impoverished, rundown cities. The rise of the computer and the IT revolution seemed to make things even worse. Now that everyone could easily work from home and do their shopping online, no one would ever settle again for a small, gardenless apartment that had little more attraction than its proximity to work, shops and bars. A great migration to the mainly rural provinces of Drenthe and Zeeland was predicted. The exodus would continue, reducing the cities to poverty, their land prices plummeting.

In the twenty-first century, Dutch cities are flourishing as never before. The Amsterdam population broke with the previous trend in 1985, and the capital's population has been steadily growing again ever since. The same applies to most historic cities in the Netherlands. People suddenly wanted to live in cities again. More and more they preferred a small but expensive second-hand home in an unsafe urban environment over a Saxon farm

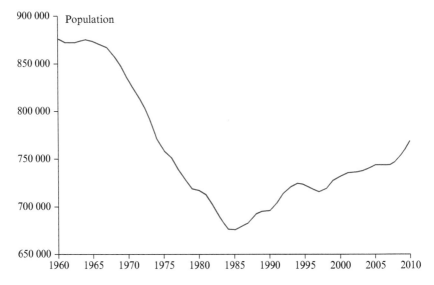

Source: *Atlas voor Gemeenten* based on Municipal Personal Records Data/CBS Statistics
Netherlands.

Figure 2.1   Decline and growth in Amsterdam, 1960–2010

in the countryside of Drenthe or a large, newly built house in the young
city of Almere. Edward Glaeser called it the paradox of urban triumph:
decreasing transportation costs in combination with an increasing population density. This chapter presents the consequences of this reversal for the
development of land prices.

THE MONOCENTRIC CITY

Cities exist by the grace of the presence of facilities with high fixed costs,
such as a bridge over a river, a harbour, a marketplace, a concert building
or a large office building that offers jobs to many. These kinds of facilities
cannot be cut into equal pieces to be distributed over the country. They
are only cost-effective if the market is sufficiently large. By living near to
one another, people can share the costs: the city is the scale that makes it
attractive to produce them.

So, the city has something to offer that makes people want to live there.
In a traditional monocentric city, these are the jobs that can be found in
the Central Business District (CBD). Being close to that CBD saves travel

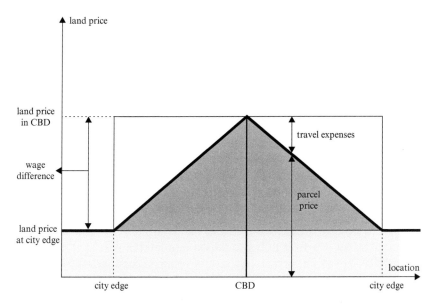

Figure 2.2   Land prices in the monocentric city

time and makes people prepared to pay more for a dwelling. As a consequence of the high land prices in the direct neighbourhood of the CBD, people have smaller homes, either on smaller plots or in high-rise building blocks.

The essence of the monocentric city is reflected in Figure 2.2. The distance to the CBD (on the horizontal axis) has been set against the land prices (on the vertical axis). All the jobs can be found in the CBD. Working in the city is more profitable than working in the countryside outside the edge of the city. On the other hand, however, living in the city centre is more expensive than living at its edge. At the end of the day, in a spatial equilibrium people should be equally well off, otherwise there would be an incentive to move. The wage difference between the city and the countryside should, therefore, always be equal to the sum of the higher land price in the city and the travel expenses to the CBD. Close to the CBD, the travel expenses are nil, and the difference in land price equals the difference in wages. At the edge of the city, the land price is as high as in the countryside, so the travel expenses to the CBD are exactly the same as the wage difference. The higher the travel expenses per kilometre, the steeper the land price curve in the city. An important implication of this reasoning is that cities expand when the travel expenses go down or the wage difference goes up. This explains an important part of the growth of cities since the Industrial Revolution. A simple rule of thumb is that the size of a city is roughly equal to the distance that can be travelled within an hour.

In Figure 2.2, the orange and yellow sections represent the city's total wage surplus: the wage difference between city and countryside (vertically) multiplied by the total population (horizontally, from the left-hand to the right-hand edge of the city). In the city centre – where all the work can be found – the land price difference between the city and the countryside is equal to this wage surplus. A part of this surplus is spent on travel expenses, which is shown in the yellow sections. The city's total net benefit – the total wage surplus minus the travel expenses to the CBD – must then be equal to the orange sections. These orange sections represent the city's total land value surplus compared to the countryside. So the city's net benefit is equal to the land value surplus. In other words: in theory, the net benefit is fully capitalised into land prices. That is why the land prices are an important indicator of urban success.

In the one-dimensional city in Figure 2.2, the land value surplus is exactly 50 per cent of the total wage surplus whilst the other half is swallowed up by travel expenses. In a two-dimensional circular city with the same characteristics, two-thirds of the total wage surplus would be travel expenses. Hence, in a monocentric city whose attraction would purely be a wage premium for working in the CBD, the land value surplus would be equal to one-third of the wage surplus.

Now, what happens if the wage premium is raised by one euro? The value of agricultural land and the travel expenses – the yellow and green sections – remain unchanged. This means that all the land prices in the city would have to rise by one euro. The wage raise would then be fully absorbed by the price of land. The city will also expand a little, but the contribution of the land value surplus to this can be ignored, since the land price at the edge of the city is equal to the price of agricultural land.

THE MONOCENTRIC CONSUMER CITY

A monocentric city's basis of existence is not necessarily the wage premium in the CBD (the city as a production city), but may also be the public facilities located in its city centre (the city as a consumer city), or a combination of both. A city with a centre that appeals through its public facilities can also be regarded as a monocentric city. Figure 2.2 can, therefore, also be used to analyse the functioning of that type of consumer city, if we substitute the CBD with a public good. The public facility's user benefit plays the same role as the wage premium in the city versus the countryside. It doesn't cost people anything to use this public good, but the further they have to travel to use it, the less they appreciate it.

City dwellers must travel to this public good to benefit from it. The land price difference in the city centre now reflects their willingness to pay for it. A household moving from the countryside to the city centre gives up exactly this amount for being able to use the public good. A household that lives further away from the public good should have a discount on the land price at the value of the travel expenses in order to be equally as well off as the household in the city centre. At the edge of the city, the appreciation for the public good is exactly equal to the travel expenses, so it is no longer worthwhile to use it. The surplus of the city is, in this case, equal to the difference between the total value that the households in the city attach to the use of the local public good, minus the travel expenses, minus the costs of the public good. The total value comprises the yellow and orange sections, and the total travel expenses the yellow ones. What remains are the red sections: the land value surplus. The surplus of the city is thus equal to the land value surplus minus the costs of the public good. That is exactly equal to the profit of the city developer. In theory, therefore, developers will enter until the profit equals zero. In that case, the land value surplus must equal the costs of the public good: the Henry George Theorem (HGT). The developer is thus not only encouraged to supply an efficient array of public goods, but also has the means to do so. The number of cities that arise through the competition between developers is also socially efficient, since the surplus of an extra city within the existing equilibrium does not outweigh its costs.

FROM HOUSE PRICES TO LAND PRICES

So, land prices contain important information about the characteristics of a living environment and its value. They are, therefore, also of great importance for social cost–benefit analyses and spatial policy. The knowledge of land prices in the Netherlands is nevertheless very limited. There is no publicly accessible information on land prices in the Netherlands. Municipalities do perform calculations on the basis of which transactions with project developers take place, but they cautiously keep these calculations to themselves.

There is more information available about house prices: at the NVM (Dutch Association of Real Estate Brokers), for instance. The land value can be derived from those house prices. The basis to do so is a simple empirical framework through which the house prices can be unravelled into individual characteristics of the house (dwelling specific amenities), on the one hand, and environmental characteristics (location specific amenities), on the other hand. The price of a house then is the sum of a series of implicit prices for the parts that together make up the house as it is. A buyer will be prepared to pay more for a house with a garage than for a house without one. The price difference offers an indication of the value of the garage. Furthermore, the buyer will tend to pay less for a house next to an airstrip than for a house a few kilometres away. The lower price compensates for the noise pollution as well as the risk of an air crash.

This simple insight forms the basis of the hedonic price method. The hedonic price method explains the variance in house prices from the variance in the characteristics of a dwelling and its surroundings. Based on the house prices and their variance, this hedonic price method can be used to gain insight into Dutch land prices. A hedonic price comparison was used to establish which part of the difference in house prices is determined by the individual characteristics of the dwelling, and which part by the value of the land underneath – the price for its location. For the analysis we used, amongst other things, the size of the dwelling, the presence of a garage, the type of dwelling (detached, semi-detached, terraced, etc.) and the plot surface area. When house prices are explained in this way, we gain insight into whatever the consumers in the margin are prepared to pay for the characteristics of a house. For subsequent analyses, it is primarily the willingness to pay for an extra square metre of plot surface that is relevant.

Table 2.1 shows the effects of the characteristics of a dwelling on house prices. The analysis is based on transactions over the period 1985–2007. As the prices for an extra square metre of land cannot unambiguously be determined for apartments these were not included in our analysis. A total of more than one million transactions took place during this period, on the basis of which the analysis was conducted. The analyses were performed separately for each province, after which the weighted average effects were reported. Real prices were expressed in 2007 levels by taking into account the general price rise of dwellings in the relevant province.

A coefficient of 0.01 indicates that the price of a dwelling increases by 1 per cent if the explanatory variable changes by one unit. The results show that the price of a dwelling rises 53 per cent when its living surface doubles; the absence of a central heating system leads to a 14 per cent lower price; the presence of a garage results in an 8 per cent higher price, a carport in 5 per cent more, etc. Last, we looked at the effect of the age of the dwelling. All effects apply to dwellings that were built after 1990. Especially houses that were built in the 1930s were relatively attractive (taking into account the inferior state of maintenance that is characteristic of these houses, which makes them cheaper than houses built in the last two decades of the 1900s). Houses built in the post-war era are relatively cheap.

Table 2.1   Explaining variation in housing prices (in logarithms)

Dwelling's characteristic	Effect
Log living surface (in m²)	0.53
No central heating	−0.14
Semi-detached	−0.12
End house	0.21
Terraced house	−0.21
Own parking space	0.02
Carport	0.05
Garage	0.08
Carport and garage	0.10
Double garage	0.09
Built before 1906	−0.11
Built between 1906 and 1930	−0.16
Built between 1931 and 1944	−0.12
Built between 1945 and 1959	−0.17
Built between 1960 and 1970	−0.17
Built between 1971 and 1980	−0.13
Built between 1981 and 1990	−0.08

Notes:
Except for the living surface, all variables are dummies (0–1 variables). Furthermore, in all regressions PC-4 specific effects for plot surface, month dummies for the month of transaction and year dummies for the year of transaction were incorporated. The transactions concern only ground-bound dwellings for the period 1985–2007.

Source: Own calculations on the basis of data provided by the NVM (Dutch Association of Real Estate Brokers).

GEOGRAPHY OF LAND PRICES

Figure 2.3 shows the derived land prices at PC-4 level (4-digit ZIP-code level). The data relate to the period 1985–2007. Prices are expressed in constant prices of 2007. Outlined are the 22 metropolitan areas (MAs) defined by CBS Statistics Netherlands, where 50 per cent of the Dutch population live. The land prices in the MAs are significantly higher than in other areas. The land prices in the MAs in the Randstad area in western Holland are also clearly higher than those in the MAs in the rest of the country. To give a sense of the order of magnitude: in the Amsterdam MA, the average land price per square metre is EUR 700; in Utrecht it is almost EUR 400; in the MAs such as Arnhem, Tilburg and Leeuwarden it is around EUR 200 and in Heerlen, Geleen/Sittard it is EUR 100.

Land prices in strongly urbanised areas are significantly higher than

Land prices per m²

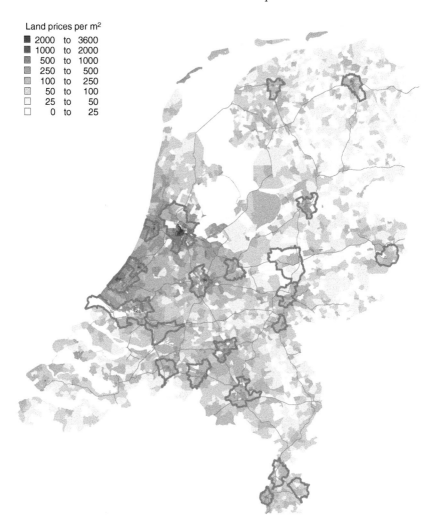

Notes:
In black: MA boundary.

Source: Own calculations on the basis of the data provided by the NVM (Dutch
Association of Real Estate Brokers).

*Figure 2.3   Land prices in the Netherlands strongly diverge (PC-4 level,
              prices of 2007)*

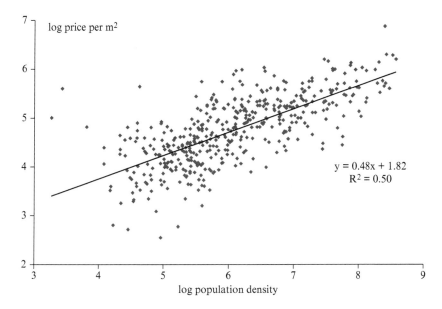

y = 0.48x + 1.82
R² = 0.50

Source: Own calculations on the basis of data provided by the NVM (Dutch Association of Real Estate Brokers) and CBS Statistics Netherlands.

Figure 2.4 *The greater population density in a municipality, the higher the land price*

those in the more peripheral urbanised areas and the countryside. A higher land price goes hand in hand with a higher population density, as is illustrated by Figure 2.4. Wherever land is expensive, the plots will be smaller and high-rise blocks will be more profitable. This results in a negative correlation between land prices and plot sizes, as shown in Figure 2.5. Both Figure 2.4 and Figure 2.5 show that a 1 per cent rise in land price leads to a 2 per cent incline in the population density and a more than 1 per cent decline in plot size.

It should be noted, however, that in this analysis we exclusively looked at ground-bound dwellings to determine the land prices, so that we only have information about the plot surfaces of those specific dwellings. The value of land on which apartment buildings were built is, due to the high rise, on average higher than the value of land with a standard dwelling. The value of land prices in city centres – where there are relatively more high-rise blocks – is underestimated in our method. The actual relationship between land prices and distance to city centres is, therefore, likely to be steeper than reported here.

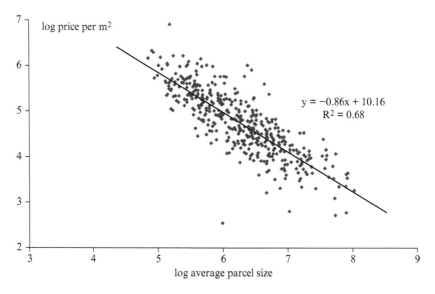

Source: Own calculations on the basis of the data provided by the NVM (Dutch
Association of Real Estate Brokers).

Figure 2.5   The greater the plot surface, the lower the land price

There are also great differences between the cities. In most Dutch cities, the square-metre price for a dwelling in the city centre is higher than for one on the outskirts. Figure 2.6 illustrates this for the metropolitan areas of Amsterdam, Utrecht, Groningen, and Nijmegen. A spot in the centre is much more expensive than a location at the edge of the city.

The theoretically predicted pattern of land prices in the monocentric city seems to be reasonably correct for the Netherlands. People are clearly willing to pay more to be able to live near a city centre. On top of that comes the unmistakable Randstad bonus – non-urban areas within the agglomeration of western Holland are more expensive than the non-urban areas elsewhere in the country – which does not logically follow from the monocentric city model, but this probably has to do with the proximity of relatively large cities and the variance in the appeal of the different cities in the Netherlands (see also Chapter 3).

Apart from the land prices, there is another way to characterise a mono-centric city, namely on the basis of commuter flows. After all, people living within the boundaries of an urban agglomeration travel to the city centre in order to work in the CBD or to benefit from the advantages of the public facilities located there. Commuter flows provide the information

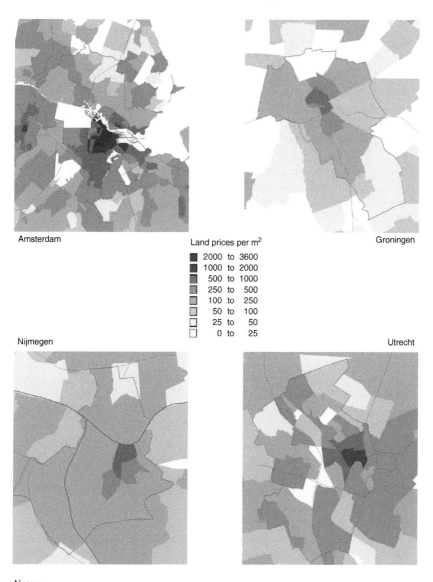

Notes:
In black: MA boundary.

Source: Own calculations on the basis of the data provided by the NVM (Dutch
Association of Real Estate Brokers).

Figure 2.6   *The closer to the city centre, the higher the land price (price*
level of 2007)

that is needed to see how far the appeal of the city centre ranges. Figure 2.7 shows the commuter flows between the municipalities in the Netherlands. For ease of interpretation, only the flows of more than 1000 workers are included. The colours show whether, on balance, workers travel to or from each municipality. The boundaries of the MAs are also indicated. Most MAs are clearly working areas; they fulfil the role of the CBD in the monocentric model of the city. The definition of an MA underestimates the economic significance of the core municipality within it. In economic terms, Zwolle, Groningen, and Leeuwarden clearly range much further than the boundaries of their MAs. In the province of Limburg we also see considerable commuting between the three MAs of Maastricht, Geleen/Sittard, and Heerlen, making it a multi-centric integrated urban area. The cities in the triangle of Breda–'s-Hertogenbosch–Eindhoven in Brabant province also seem to be monocentric cities by themselves. In the Randstad area, the core municipalities of Utrecht, Amsterdam, Rotterdam and The Hague are unmistakable. The Hague and Rotterdam are mutually strongly integrated – far more than Utrecht and Amsterdam. The significance of Amsterdam covers the entire hexagon of Hoorn–Castricum–Zandvoort–Warmond–Hilversum–Almere. At the southern perimeter of Amsterdam, the strong integration with the municipality of Haarlemmermeer can be recognised. The latter is clearly a work-providing municipality, owing to Schiphol airport, which is located there.

Irrespective of the spatial distribution of the land prices, in the light of the discussion about whether or not the importance of cities is declining it is also interesting to take a look at the development of real house prices over time, for which purpose we adjusted house prices for the rise in the consumer price level. To do so, we used a hedonic price model comparable to the one we described earlier. In order to map out the long-term dynamics, we added a separate linear time trend for each municipality. This time trend reflects the differences in the rise of real house prices after adjusting them for their characteristics. The results are presented in Figure 2.8. The rises comprise representational rises in the value of the buildings as well as in the land. The regional differences in price rises are primarily the result of variances in the development of land prices, since the value of buildings is determined by construction costs. These construction costs are similar throughout the country. The development of land prices is, therefore, even more divergent than that of house prices.

It appeared that, indeed, the appreciation for the city and the importance of the Randstad area strongly increased between 1985 and 2007. In comparison with the north-eastern part of the province of Groningen, house prices in Amsterdam more than doubled during those years. As for land prices, these differences are even greater. In the northern part of the

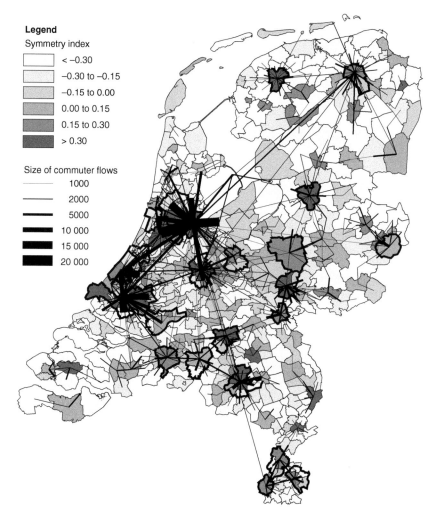

Legend

Symmetry index

	< −0.30
	−0.30 to −0.15
	−0.15 to 0.00
	0.00 to 0.15
	0.15 to 0.30
	> 0.30

Size of commuter flows

	1000
	2000
	5000
	10 000
	15 000
	20 000

Notes:
In black: MA boundary.

Source: Own calculations on the basis of the micro-data provided by CBS Statistics Netherlands.

Figure 2.7   Commuter flows strongly focused on core municipalities in MAs

Growth in %
■ 6 to 7.2
■ 5 to 6
■ 4 to 5
░ 3 to 4
  0 to 3
  no data

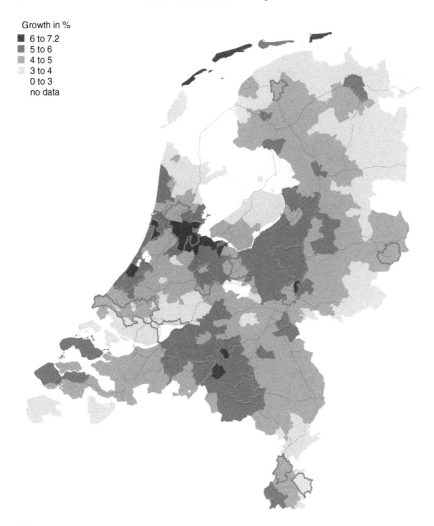

Notes:
In black: MA boundary.

Source: Own calculations on the basis of the data provided by the NVM (Dutch
Association of Real Estate Brokers).

*Figure 2.8   Stronger rise in house prices in urban areas than in the
            countryside (growth trend per municipality, 1985–2007)*

Randstad area, the increase in value was greater than in the southern part. In the city triangle of Breda–'s-Hertogenbosch–Eindhoven and the inner cities of Maastricht, Groningen and The Hague, prices also rose significantly. Noticeably greater price rises occurred in parts of the Gelderland and in the west of the Friesland provinces. The land prices in Figure 2.3 for the urbanised areas with a rapid growth of house prices are, therefore, an underestimate of the true 2007 real prices; in our adjustment of the land prices we only took into account the general price rise per province and not the differences in trends within the provinces. In other words, land prices in cities such as Groningen and Leeuwarden – where they rose relatively quickly – are underestimated, whereas land prices in the rural areas of the Groningen and Friesland provinces are overestimated.

THE FIVE MOST IMPORTANT CONCLUSIONS

After a long period of decline Dutch cities have been in vogue again since 1985.

Land prices in the Randstad area are far higher than in the peripheral areas; in cities they are higher than in their surrounding areas; and higher in inner cities than at the edge of the city.

The price of land in Amsterdam city centre is 200 times as high as that in the countryside of East-Groningen.

This price difference more than doubled between 1985 and 2007. The importance of location has, therefore, grown considerably.

Commuter flows in the Netherlands reveal a star-shaped pattern that is typical of urban agglomerations.

FURTHER READING

Jan K. Brueckner, Jacques-François Thisse and Yves Zenou, 1999, Why is central Paris rich and Detroit poor? An amenity-based theory, *European Economic Review*, 43(1), 91–107.

Jane Jacobs, 1969, *The Economy of Cities*, Random House, New York.

Arthur O'Sullivan, 2009, *Urban Economics*, McGraw Hill, Boston.

Jennifer Roback, 1982, Wages, rents and the quality of life, *Journal of Political Economy*, 90(6), 1257–78.

Petra Visser and Frank van Dam, 2006, *De prijs van de plek*, Ruimtelijk Planbureau, NAI Uitgevers, The Hague.

3. The dynamics of the Dutch system of cities

Urbanization is a process of population concentration. It proceeds in two ways: the multiplication of points of concentration and the increase in size of individual concentrations.

Hope Eldridge Tisdale, 1942

When you look at a seventeenth-century map of the Netherlands, you will be able to recognise a lot of its current urban structure: it will take no effort to find Leyden, Dort, Gouda, Breda, 's-Hertogenbosch, Gorcum and Delft. The smaller cities of, for example, Bodegraven, Nieuwcoop, Boscoop, Diemen and Duivendrecht are also outlined. The river-based cities of Bommel, Montfoort, Ysselsteyn, Willemstat, Geertrudenberch, Duierstede Wijck and Culemborch even had serious fortifications in those days. However, if you are trying to find Zoetermeer and Amstelveen, you will not be able to find them. Nor is there any trace of Almere, Haarlemmermeer, or Emmeloord – where the sea was wet as wet could be. As for the rest, most of the cities and villages have a long history. The Dutch urban pattern is reasonably stable. Once in a while something new emerges, but in general the structure seems to be an irreversible fact – even though this is a relative conclusion. Almost all of the river-based cities have lost their economic value. Apart from its fortifications and the church steeple of Bommel that the Dutch sing about, there is little to remind us of its glorious past. The boundaries of Amsterdam have since reached those of Diemen and Duivendrecht. The cities of Zoetermeer, Amstelveen, and Hoofddorp have grown considerably. It takes quite some time and effort for a village or city to really disappear. The relative size of cities, however, is very agile.

Figure 3.1 documents this phenomenon, using the development of the number of inhabitants in the 25 largest cities of the Netherlands during the period 1849–1971 based on their municipal boundaries. These have changed quite considerably in the course of time. Wherever possible, we used definitions that remained the same over the entire period. The top four were the same over the entire period, although Amsterdam's relative lead over its pursuers strongly diminished. Fifth in 1849, Leiden had a

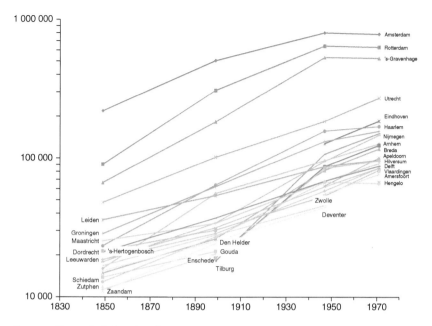

Source: Own calculations based on censuses.

Figure 3.1   The relative size of cities is very agile

completely different fate; in the year 2009 it was barely able to hold on to its ranking in the top 25. Quite the opposite applies to Eindhoven, fifth in 2009 but which only entered the top 25 in 1947. The largest cities in 1849 were, almost without exception, cities that were located by the water, with their own harbour and a distinct commercial function. Fifty years later we see the first, tentative rise of industrial cities such as Enschede and Tilburg and, after 1950, Eindhoven, Hilversum and Apeldoorn. By that time, many of the Hanse towns had completely disappeared from the group of largest cities. It appeared that 's-Hertogenbosch would share that same fate, but as of 1947 it was on the up again. In recent history, the cities of Almere, Apeldoorn, Amersfoort, Haarlemmermeer and Zoetermeer emerged as important centres of urban growth. The dynamics can also be illustrated by the transitions in the municipalities' rankings between 1849 and 1971 (see Table 3.1).

In Table 3.1, the municipalities are classified according to their size and divided into ten equal groups (deciles) of cities. The first decile, therefore, comprises the 10 per cent smallest municipalities in a year, the second decile the next 10 per cent, etc. More than 20 per cent of the cities

Table 3.1   Strong transition dynamics of municipalities between 1849 and 1971

Decile in 1849	Decile in 1971									
	1	2	3	4	5	6	7	8	9	10
1	34	12	8	2	1	0	0	0	0	0
2	10	15	6	13	7	3	2	2	0	0
3	4	8	14	5	7	6	9	3	1	1
4	3	4	6	12	3	8	10	7	4	1
5	0	6	7	4	10	9	1	10	5	7
6	0	2	1	8	9	7	7	11	7	5
7	2	4	3	6	4	4	9	4	13	9
8	3	3	3	4	4	10	8	2	14	7
9	1	3	3	3	3	7	7	12	6	13
10	0	1	7	1	10	4	5	7	8	15

Notes:
The upper left-hand cell indicates that 34 municipalities belonged to the 10 per cent smallest municipalities in the Netherlands in both 1849 and 1971.

Source: Own calculations based on censuses.

in this period of over 120 years stayed in the same decile; 55 per cent of the municipalities moved more than one decile. In 1849, more than 90 per cent of the municipalities had a population of less than 5000. In 1971, this still applied to only 55 per cent: a reflection of the urbanisation trend that followed the rapid industrialisation in the nineteenth century. Do these strong dynamics of Dutch cities have a structure? And, if so, what are the implications of this uncertainty about the future development of a city for land prices and spatial planning policy?

CHANCE AND ZIPF'S LAW

Table 3.2 presents the results of a statistical analysis of the information in Figure 3.1. The first row shows the average population growth rate of the 100 largest municipalities in 1971 for four periods. On average, the Dutch municipalities underwent growth in all periods, somewhat more rapidly between 1889 and 1971 than in the periods before and after. The second row reflects the connection between the municipality's size and its growth rate. A coefficient of 1 means that a 10 per cent larger municipality grew 10 per cent more quickly over that entire period. A negative

Table 3.2   Very weak correlation between the growth and size of municipalities

	1849–1889	1889–1930	1930–1971	1980–2009
Annual growth (in %)	1.05	2.56	2.23	0.72
Correlation of growth – initial size	−0.0001	−0.0063	−0.0080	−0.0046
Standard deviation (in %)	0.83	1.66	1.21	0.83

Notes:
The analysis relates to the 100 largest municipalities in 1971.

Source: Own calculations based on censuses for the period 1849–1971, and data provided by CBS Netherlands Statistics for the period 1980–2009.

coefficient says that larger municipalities are in fact growing more slowly. The reported coefficients were close to zero, which means that the growth rate of a municipality is virtually independent of its current size. So, the results achieved in the past offer no guarantees for the future. The third row shows the standard deviation of the average annual growth rate. A standard deviation of 1 per cent means that the population number is, on average, approximately 1 per cent greater or smaller after one year than the average growth. This means that, over a period of 50 years, a municipality is on average 7 per cent greater or smaller than would be expected on the basis of the trend.

This outcome – i.e. that the growth of cities is virtually independent of their current size – also applies to businesses. For businesses, their current size says nothing about chances and threats in the near future either. The only difference between cities and businesses is that the uncertainty for businesses is actually far greater than for cities – by up to a factor of ten. Xavier Gabaix demonstrates that the independence of a city's growth from its current size automatically leads to a highly specific form of the distribution of cities' sizes (see further reading). That form is known as the rank size rule, or Zipf's Law: the largest city in the country is twice as big as the second city, three times as big as the country's third city, four times as big as the fourth, etc. This law results in a skewed distribution of cities as well as a skewed distribution of the population over the cities: a few large cities comprise a disproportionately large part of the population. Mathematically, this law leads to a linear relation between the logarithms of the population numbers and the cities' ranking – in its purest form even with a slope of –1.

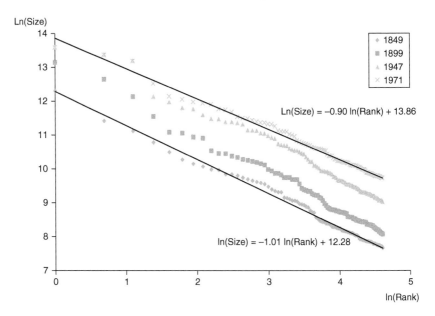

Source: Own calculations based on censuses.

Figure 3.2   The rank size rule took a more level route for the 100 largest cities (1949–1971)

ZIPF'S LAW FOR THE NETHERLANDS

Figure 3.2 shows the relationship between the size and ranking of cities in the Netherlands. From this simple graph, a couple of relevant stylised facts characterising the structure of the urban system in the Netherlands can be derived: Figure 3.2 shows the relationship between the size and ranking of the 100 largest municipalities in the Netherlands over time, based on information from censuses. The unit of measurement here is not a well-defined urban agglomeration, but a municipality. However, the municipalities of Vlaardingen and Schiedam have meanwhile become as good as fully integrated in the built-up area of Rotterdam; Wassenaar, Leidschendam and Voorburg in that of The Hague; and Amstelveen, Diemen and Duivendrecht in the city of Amsterdam. The use of municipalities instead of agglomerations thus results in a flatter distribution, as the population of the suburbs are not included. The figure shows that Zipf's Law held in its purest form 150 years ago, and almost perfectly: the slope is practically –1. Over the course of time, the slope varied. Up to the start of the 1900s, during industrialisation, it rose in order to subsequently fall gradually until

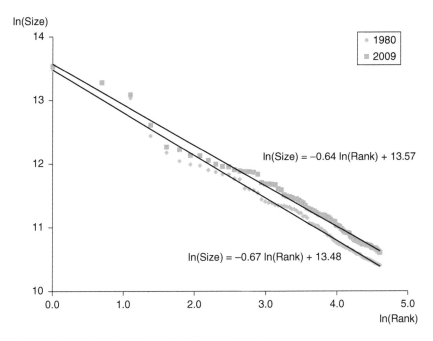

Source: Own calculations on the basis CBS Statline data.

Figure 3.3   *The rank size rule took a more level route for the 100 largest*
              cities in a recent period also (1980–2009)

it reaches a value that is substantially smaller than one. The rank size rule thus flattened; in other words, the distribution of Dutch municipalities according to their size became more level in the course of the last century. This was driven by a process of a gradual growth of the small and medium-sized cities and the relatively limited growth of, particularly, Amsterdam. Rotterdam and The Hague did undergo relatively strong growth during this period. The trend towards the levelling of the distribution continued, also after 1971, as is shown by Figure 3.3. The data in Figure 3.3 cannot be simply compared with those in Figure 3.2, however, since they use different definitions of municipality. This explains the great decline of the slope between 1971 and 1980. Although the analysis presented here is based on the population numbers per municipality and not per agglomeration – which leads to a lower Zipf coefficient – other studies also showed that the Dutch distribution of city sizes was relatively even. Incidentally, the trend towards levelling out can also be seen in other countries.

   In many countries, the capital does not fit the rank size rule: that city is usually much larger, often as a consequence of the government's monopoly of power. This monopoly places a substantial flow of tax income at the disposal of civil servants of the government, which can then be spent on the adornment of the royal residence. As can be expected, this phenomenon, therefore, occurs most strongly in countries that are ruled by an absolute monarch and with a limited separation of powers, or in countries that had these for a very long time. The positions of Athens in Greece and Paris in France are obvious examples. The capitals of many developing countries are also much larger than Zipf's Law would predict. Be that as it may, this phenomenon does not occur in the Netherlands.

Although Zipf's Law has a baffling general validity, in many countries it only applies roughly. A country where it does apply practically perfectly in its purest form is the United States. Many countries, however, deviate from the pattern. Kenneth Rosen and Mitchel Resnick (see further reading) demonstrated that Zipf's Law in its purest form can be refuted for 26 of 44 countries; later studies confirmed this picture. However, in 80 per cent of cases the slope was found to be between 0.70 and 1.20 (see Figure 3.4). The Zipf coefficient of 0.64 for 2009 (see Figure 3.3), therefore, strongly deviates from what was found for other countries.

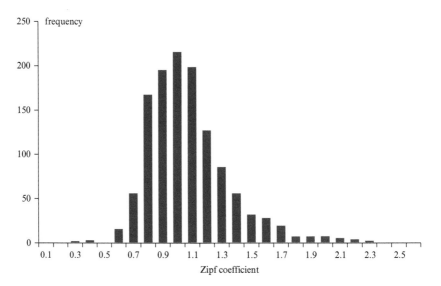

Source: Meta-analysis by Peter Mulder and Henri de Groot (see further reading).

Figure 3.4   Wide distribution of Zipf coefficients between countries and over time

THE MYSTERY OF ZIPF'S LAW

Jan de Vries outlined how the Dutch city system in 1500 was less developed than that of the Belgian cities that were highly prosperous at the time (see further reading); only Utrecht managed to live up to the status of a large, central city in this period. The place that we now call Amsterdam was primarily marshland at that time. The rapid economic development in the centuries that followed led to a structure that, even as early as 1650, strongly resembled Zipf's Law. A sound, generally acceptable theoretical explanation for the fact that the growth of cities is independent of their size, and thus for Zipf's Law, has not been found – so there is no proper explanation for deviations from that law either.

Important building blocks for an explanation can be found in Paul Krugman's theory of the New Economic Geography. Krugman's theory is based on a trade-off between transportation costs and scale benefits. Concentration of production in one spot has the advantage of the optimal exploitation of scale benefits. The price that must be paid for this is that goods need to be shipped to other markets. Labourers and companies are free to choose their location. Even in the simplest case with two regions, the model is characterised by multiple equilibria. In two equilibria, the production is concentrated in one of the two regions, and in a third equilibrium there is a distribution of the production over both locations. History plays a role in these models. The chance that a great region is able to hold on to the industry is great, since the large home market turns the region into an appealing location. But coincidence and expectations also play a major part. A chance decision by an entrepreneur to set up business somewhere can induce a self-enhancing process so that a small region outgrows itself. The more the transportation costs decline, the greater the chance is of an equilibrium with a full concentration of production in one location as a consequence of the companies' and workers' relocation behaviour. After all, the scale benefits will outweigh the transportation costs.

In this setting, one of the interesting characteristics of New Economic Geography models is that small changes can have huge and permanent effects. A minor subsidy granted to one manufacturing company can induce a process whereby the region can eventually take a dominant position in the economy, hence the fascination of policy makers for this theory. At the same time, however, this theory also underlines the importance of coincidences. Paul Krugman mentioned the carpet industry in Dalton as an example: beforehand, the location of this industry was completely unpredictable, but once the choice was made, it led to a self-enhancing process with a successful cluster of specialised activities as a result. The history of Philips is, in a certain way, similar. The choice by Philips to start in Eindhoven rather than in Helmond is still said to have been mostly a chance decision: the rest is history. Such successes, however, mainly allow for explanations afterwards. The step towards efficient policy that aims to attract and hold on to economic activity is considerable. Experiences with the industrial policies of the 1980s give little reason for hope.

Why is the Dutch distribution of city sizes so much flatter than elsewhere? A possible explanation is the specific shape of the Dutch delta. This shape has led to the emergence of two relatively large cities, Amsterdam and Rotterdam, which developed rather independently of one another until the middle of the 1800s, separated as they were by an inland sea called the Haarlemmermeer. The port activities are still strictly divided between the two separate cities, both having a seaport as well as an airport. The reclamation of the Haarlemmermeer sea around 1850 explains the decline of the city of Leiden, situated on the edge of the Haarlemmermeer sea at that time. The reclamation closed off this city's access to the sea and thereby an important source of income from trade.

The explanation may also lie in the political balance of power in the Netherlands and the organisation of its public administration, as well as the special position of the capital in these. Thorbecke's 1848 constitution, with a division of power between the central government, provinces and municipalities, is strongly inclined towards distributive justice. Whereas in other countries the primate city is, due to the government's monopoly of power, greater than predicted by Zipf's Law, Amsterdam is rather smaller. This is in line with the fact that, since 1848, the Netherlands has not had an absolute monarchy and, even more so, that Amsterdam has never been the centre of government. Up to a certain point the spatial planning is a reflection of this distributive justice: all cities had to have equal opportunities. This led to the strict regulation of new building developments and restrictions to new supply in the housing market. Successful cities with a favourable specialisation pattern were thus confronted with a limitation to their growth potential. Characteristic of Dutch administrative relations is the policy aimed at new centres of urban growth and the constraints on large cities' expansion, for instance by protecting the 'Green Heart' (*Groene Hart*), the sparsely populated rural area within the Randstad area that was designated a national park in 2004.

The uncertainty about the future development of individual cities has had major implications for land value and the value of the properties built on it. The consequences of the closure of the coal mines for the value of properties in Heerlen and Geleen/Sittard are still noticeable today. The same goes for the demise of the textile industry and the house and land prices in Enschede and Helmond. It is important to realise that investments in buildings do have a very nasty characteristic: they are irreversible. If a location loses its appeal, an investment cannot simply be undone. Dennis Capozza and Robert Helsley analysed the consequences of this irreversibility (see further reading). In the construction of buildings, the difference in value between the built-on and a vacant plot should be equal to the construction costs of the buildings, for if the difference in value is smaller, the owner would have been smart not to build and if, conversely, the difference in value is greater, the owner could always decide to build after all. The option to do so at a later stage inflates the price of a vacant plot to the price of that same plot with buildings but, in that case, minus the construction costs. A great part of the value of agricultural land in the direct vicinity of the city exists in the optional value of erecting buildings on it later on.

If the city starts to decline, this equality no longer applies to the entire city. At the edge of the city, in the marginal locations, the difference in value between the built-on area and the vacant land will then be smaller than the construction costs: so, no owner in his right mind would decide to build on the vacant land. Since, however, their investments are irreversible, owners do not have the possibility to go back on their first decision. That makes it more difficult to distinguish between the value of land and the value of buildings.

THE DYNAMICS OF CITIES AND INDUSTRY STRUCTURE

The structure of industry in a country is the result of supply and demand factors. On the demand side, an important part is played by the income elasticity of various spending categories: the elasticity of the demand for foodstuffs is low, and for services it is high. The wealthier people become, the more their spending shifts from food to material products to services. On the supply side, the great productivity rise in agriculture and the small productivity rise in most service industries are important. These factors result in a continuing decline of employment in agriculture, while employment in manufacturing first rises before subsequently falling again and the employment in services continually grows. This pattern occurs worldwide. A second factor is international trade. Trade leads to specialisation based on comparative benefits. The Netherlands has a comparative benefit in trade and transport, due to its unique geographical location and its long tradition as a broker and connector in the international exchange of goods. Table 3.3 shows this shift in employment for the period 1993–2003. Even for this short period, it confirms the picture of a relatively small and

Table 3.3   *Employment shifts from agriculture and manufacturing*
              industry to services

	Magnitude in 2003 ($\times$ 1000)	Contribution in 2003 (in %)	Annual growth 1993–2003 (in %)
Agriculture and fishery	97	1.4	−0.1
Manufacturing and construction industry	960	18.3	−0.7
Construction industry	389	5.6	0.9
Commercial services industry	3243	46.6	3.2
Non-commercial services industry	2344	33.7	3.4
Total	6957	100.0	2.5

Source: Own calculations on the basis of CBS Statline data.

shrinking manufacturing industry and a relatively large and growing services industry. Although, in terms of employment, the commercial services industry was still the greatest industry, the non-commercial services industry grew most rapidly. These industries potentially have a different pattern of spatial concentration. What are the consequences of this shift from agriculture to the services industry for this spatial specialisation pattern and the development of cities?

In order to ascertain spatial specialisation of economic activity, various measures have been developed in the literature, which are related to the notion of the location quotient. The location quotient measures the ratio between employment in a certain industry in a certain region and the contribution of that same industry to the national economy. A relatively high value of the location quotient indicates that an industry is relatively strongly overrepresented in the relevant region.

An aggregate measure for specialisation is the Hirschmann–Herfindahl index. This index is based on the differences in the regional presence of a certain industry relative to the contribution to the national employment of the regions as a whole. When these differences are great, the relevant industry is strongly concentrated in a limited number of regions. Small differences indicate that an industry is evenly divided between all regions. The minimum value of the index is 0 (perfect distribution) and a maximum value of 2 (full concentration in some regions).

Table 3.4 shows the Hirschmann–Herfindahl index for eight broad industries. The spatial aggregation level comprises 40 COROP regions.

Table 3.4   Hirschmann–Herfindahl index shows the differences in regional specialisation for 40 COROP regions in 2003

Industrial category	
Agriculture and fishery	0.020
Foodstuffs and luxury foods	0.009
Metal and electrical engineering	0.018
Retail trade	0.001
Finance	0.017
IT industry	0.035
Public administration	0.010
Culture and other services	0.003

Source: Laura de Dominicis, Raymond Florax and Henri de Groot (see further reading).

COROP regions are defined in accordance with a European standardised regional classification that, in principle, comprises a central city and its hinterland. As can be expected, retail trade in the Netherlands is almost perfectly spread over the entire country. The inevitable desirability of proximity between supply and demand in the retail trade explains the absence of spatial specialisation. The same, incidentally, applies to health care. Naturally, agriculture and fishery are strongly concentrated in a limited number of regions, as are a number of branches of manufacturing industry. The same goes for the professional services industry, financial organisations and the IT industry.

Figure 3.5 presents the location quotients of these industrial categories for the COROP regions. The location quotient for the retail trade indeed proves to hardly vary between the regions. For all other industries reported, it does. Employment in agriculture and fishery is strongly concentrated in a number of rural areas, in the labour-intensive greenhouse farms in the Westland region and in the flower industry. The metal and electrical engineering industry is concentrated around Eindhoven and, to a lesser extent, in the Twente region of the province of Overijssel and the south-west of the Friesland province. The cities of Amsterdam and Hilversum clearly have a location advantage where culture is concerned. Public administration is equally distributed over the country, with an obvious peak in and around the royal residence, The Hague. The business services industry is strongly concentrated: the financial industry in Amsterdam, and the IT industry in Utrecht. This reflects the international trend of manufacturing gradually moving away from the cities, whereas the services industry is actually moving towards it. Even in an industry

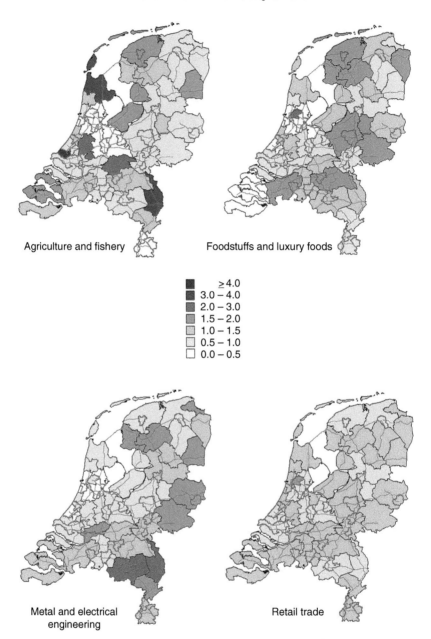

Source: Own calculations on the basis of CBS Statline data.

Figure 3.5   Location quotients per industrial category

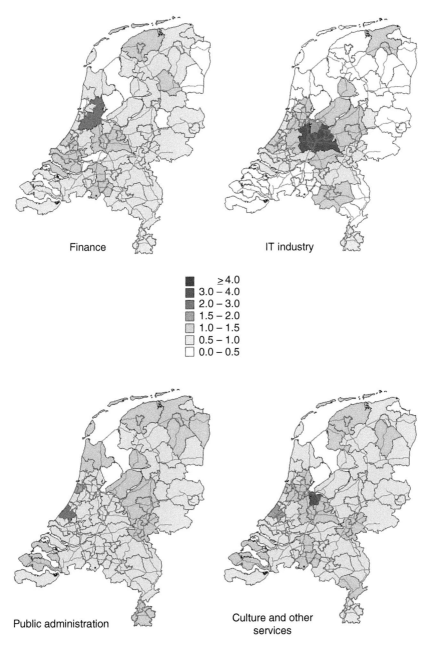

Finance

IT industry

≥ 4.0
3.0 – 4.0
2.0 – 3.0
1.5 – 2.0
1.0 – 1.5
0.5 – 1.0
0.0 – 0.5

Public administration

Culture and other services

Figure 3.5 (continued)

THE FIVE MOST IMPORTANT CONCLUSIONS

The growth and decline of cities are independent of their current size. This leads to a rather skewed distribution of cities in term of sizes, which is referred to as the rank size rule: the largest city is twice as big as the second city, three times as big as the third city, four times as big as the fourth, etc.

This distribution according to size is flatter in the Netherlands than elsewhere in the world: large cities are not so big here.

In many countries, the largest city is even greater than this rule predicts, certainly in countries with a strong central government. That does not apply to the Netherlands either: Amsterdam is smaller rather than bigger than expected.

Although their distribution according to size is reasonably stable, the cities ranking order is quite agile: the textile and mining cities rose to subsequently shrink again, the Brabant city triangle of Breda–'s-Hertogenbosch–Eindhoven has been growing strongly over the past 20 years.

The business services industry is strongly concentrated in the large cities.

---

with electronic communication as its core business – the IT industry – clustering turns out to be the order of the day. Even today, physical distance remains an obstruction for the dissemination of new ideas.

FURTHER READING

Dennis R. Capozza and Robert W. Helsley, 1990, The stochastic city, *Journal of Urban Economics*, 28(2), 187–203.

Laura de Dominicis, Raymond J.G.M. Florax and Henri L.F. de Groot, 2008, De Ruimtelijke Verdeling van Economische Activiteit: Agglomeratie- en Locatiepatronen in Nederland, *Kwartaalschrift Economie*, 5(1), 71–99.

Xavier Gabaix, 1999, Zipf's Law for cities: An explanation, *Quarterly Journal of Economics*, 114(3), 739–67.

Peter Mulder and Henri L.F. de Groot, 2008, The Economics of Zipf's Law: A meta-analysis, presentation at the ERSA conference in Lódz.

Kenneth Rosen and Mitchel Resnick, 1980, The size distribution of cities: an examination of the Pareto law and primacy, *Journal of Urban Economics*, 8(2), 165–86.

Jan de Vries (1984), *European Urbanization, 1500–1800*, Routledge Library Edition, London.

4. The production city

In almost all countries, there is a constant migration towards the towns. The large towns . . . absorb the very best blood from all the rest . . . the most enterprising, the most highly gifted, those with the highest physique and the strongest characters go there to find scope for their abilities.

Alfred Marshall, 1890

More money is earned within urban agglomerations than outside. At first glance, this could simply be explained by the uneven spatial distribution of economic activity and people. Top jobs, that require great knowledge and experience, are concentrated in the Randstad area. Routine tasks that can be performed by lower-educated staff are, by contrast, overrepresented in the rural areas. Higher-qualified workers are obviously better paid, so the average wages in the Randstad are higher. The reality, however, proves to be more complex: a random worker from the rural province of Friesland or Groningen will, on average, earn around 10 per cent more in Amsterdam. Even with equal qualifications a worker in the Randstad earns more than in rural areas. Wage differences that cannot be explained by individual characteristics of workers and companies also exist between other Dutch regions, and given the relatively small size of the Dutch economy, these differences are considerable.

What, now, explains the regional wage differences in the Netherlands? That question can be answered here with the use of the unique micro-data provided by CBS Statistics Netherlands, with information about workers and businesses. This is an import difference to earlier studies, which worked with aggregated data. Micro-data enable researchers to explore regional wage differences with otherwise similar characteristics, such as age and education. In other words, micro-data allow us to look for twins who are identical in all respects, except the location where they work. Wage differences for such twins reflect the productivity differences between locations. Through this analysis, therefore, the productivity effects of urbanisation can be mapped out.

Such productivity differences make it appealing to live close to a city. After all, the closer to the city the easier is the access to well-paid jobs in the CBD. There is, therefore, a relationship between the monocentric model of the city with its CBD and its surrounding residential neighbourhoods, on the one hand, and the existence of regional wage differences, on the other. The higher wage level in the CBD is connected to the land value surplus in the area around the CBD. If these productivity differences are the only reason for the higher land prices in the city, the Net Present Value (NPV) of the total wage difference should be one to three times as big as the land value surplus of the city as a whole (see Chapter 2). The analysis in this chapter will enable us to test this relationship.

EXPLANATIONS FOR REGIONAL WAGE AND PRODUCTIVITY DIFFERENCES

In the literature on regional wage differences, three types of explanations for these differences can be distinguished: (1) the presence of natural resources, (2) the differences in the composition of the workers' pool in the labour market, and (3) the agglomeration effects.

The agglomeration effects in particular have had great focus in the literature on productivity differences. These concern the effects that lead to workers being more productive in urbanised, densely populated areas. A company's decision to locate in a certain location determines the productivity of others. Considering that this company will not of its own accord take into account the effect of its decision on the productivity of others, these are external effects. Since these external effects correlate with the clustering of people and businesses in specific locations, they are referred to as agglomeration externalities. As individual businesses do not consider these agglomeration externalities in their location decisions, the market does not lead to the best possible result and, therefore, governmental intervention is legitimised.

Workers with different characteristics are not randomly distributed over the country. In some regions, the number of people with a certain educational level clearly deviates from the national average. The same applies for their age and the number of immigrants. Table 4.1 shows the core data for 22 Metropolitan Areas (MAs), (the so-called *Groot Stedelijke Agglomeraties*), as defined by Statistics Netherlands, as well as the weighted average of these characteristics for the area outside them. Slightly more than half of the jobs in the Netherlands are situated in one of the MAs.

This table shows that the average hourly wages differ greatly between regions, from EUR 17.90 in the countryside up to EUR 21.70 in Amsterdam: a more than 20 per cent difference. Higher-educated workers (holding a professional or academic bachelor's degree or higher) cluster in the large cities of, primarily, the Randstad area. They make up

*Table 4.1   Workers in metropolitan areas (MA) earn more and they are
higher educated than those in other areas*

MA	Higher educated (%)	Hourly wage (euro)	Part-time jobs (%)	Immigrants (%)	Women (%)	Age	Jobs per km^2
Amersfoort	42.9	19.7	45.0	6.6	50.1	41.1	826
Amsterdam	45.3	21.7	39.5	13.1	44.9	41.0	1929
Apeldoorn	31.8	18.9	44.0	4.2	47.1	40.6	296
Arnhem	38.0	19.1	48.5	5.7	50.3	41.8	886
Breda	36.4	18.4	45.0	6.8	53.0	40.6	817
Dordrecht	29.5	18.0	46.2	6.8	50.3	40.8	799
Eindhoven	42.0	19.5	40.7	7.8	46.8	40.8	1075
Enschede	36.6	17.9	47.8	7.9	51.6	40.6	568
Geleen/Sittard	30.1	18.7	42.3	5.9	43.3	42.4	631
Groningen	42.8	19.1	50.6	4.5	50.4	40.4	1081
Haarlem	37.8	19.3	49.1	7.8	54.7	41.3	1242
Heerlen	30.6	17.9	42.2	5.3	47.3	41.6	859
Leeuwarden	36.8	17.9	51.8	3.3	51.8	40.5	973
Leiden	43.0	19.6	53.9	8.4	57.3	40.3	1376
Maastricht	38.7	18.7	47.9	5.4	52.5	40.3	1460
Nijmegen	46.8	20.3	51.3	7.1	52.5	41.3	1976
Rotterdam	35.2	19.7	41.4	13.0	48.9	40.7	1675
's-Hertogenbosch	37.6	19.1	43.9	5.6	48.7	41.0	973
The Hague	45.9	21.6	37.7	13.6	47.4	40.8	2122
Tilburg	34.6	18.0	49.2	6.5	50.8	39.9	790
Utrecht	46.9	20.6	43.6	8.3	46.9	40.6	1981
Zwolle	34.4	18.0	51.4	4.4	51.7	40.8	788
Non-MA	31.7	17.9	48.1	5.4	51.5	40.7	143

Notes:
The higher educated hold a professional or academic bachelor's degree or higher.

Source: Own calculations on the basis of the micro-data provided by CBS Statistics
Netherlands.

approximately 30 per cent of the population in Heerlen, Geleen/Sittard,
Apeldoorn, Dordrecht and the non-MA areas, but peak at over 45 per cent
in Nijmegen, Utrecht, The Hague and Amsterdam. There is an evident
concentration of immigrants in the large cities in the Randstad area.
Within the densely populated Netherlands there is also a strong variation
in job density. The job density in The Hague is a factor of 14 higher than
in the non-MA areas.

Why do the higher educated prefer to dwell in certain regions? This
may be for different reasons. The classic explanation, spatial variation in

natural location benefits, plays a secondary role at the present time. Cheap access to certain resources, access to waterways or a favourable climate can, in certain regions and for certain industries, lead to a higher production level. This can result in a strong degree of spatial clustering. Due to labour migration, and the choice of certain types of studies and regional specialisation, such differences in average wages between regions will be limited in the long run. Only when the pressure on a certain region is high because of its natural resources can wages remain on a continuing higher level. However, since the closure of the mines, there are hardly any locations left that can serve as an example. The location benefit of Rotterdam at the Rhine estuary does not make this city an attractive place for the higher educated.

The second possible explanation is the agglomeration effects in the choice of location. Like London in Alfred Marshall's days, the large cities in the Netherlands attract the most capable workers. As discussed in Chapter 1, all around the world it is precisely the industries in which knowledge and innovation play a key role that settle in the large cities. In spite of the rise of the Internet, new ideas make their way the quickest through face-to-face communication. It is precisely the higher educated who play a key role in this and it is, therefore, beneficial for them to go and work in the city. The Netherlands is no exception to this pattern. The knowledge economy thus concentrates in the city. Furthermore, academic and professional universities are often located in large cities. This, in turn, makes the city an attractive location for businesses that most depend on skilled labour. Youngsters who move to the city as students, therefore, have little reason to move back to the rural areas once they have completed their education.

When the economic density in a region has increased due to the influx of businesses and their staff, agglomeration externalities can emerge. Their workings run through various mechanisms. A first source is the proximity of business to their suppliers and customers, as well as the scale of their collective activities. A second source is the so-called 'dense labour markets' in which workers and businesses are able easily to come together and where – on average – jobs and specific qualifications are better matched, which results in higher productivity. Knowledge spillover is another source of agglomeration externalities. Since knowledge is disseminated more easily in an environment with a high economic density, innovation will increase. According to Alfred Marshall, Kenneth Arrow and Paul Romer, these types of externalities arise specifically within industries because competitors that are active in each other's proximity learn from one another. Jane Jacobs, however, argues that knowledge spillover mainly occurs between industries, as it is businesses with different activities that learn from one another. Her idea is that precisely when the differences in the technology used are great, as is the case in totally different industries, there is ample room for cross-pollination. Finally, Michael Porter stresses the importance of competition between industries within regions. The key idea here is that competition leads to higher productivity when businesses with similar activities are located close to each other. In the literature, these different effects are often referred to as Marshall-Arrow-Romer (or MAR) externalities, Jacobs externalities and Porter externalities (named after the scientists associated with the effects).

When the productivity of the higher educated in a certain region is higher than the national average, businesses that have a great need of higher-educated staff tend to settle in that region. In order to attract personnel from other regions, they will be prepared to pay a higher wage (until the wages equal the marginal productivity of workers). Agglomeration externalities thus, in turn, lead to a further clustering of higher-educated people in large cities.

As the pressure on a region increases, rising prices of real estate and local facilities cause costs to rise. In equilibrium, each region is equally attractive to each worker and each business. Workers may earn more in a metropolitan area, but this advantage is cancelled out by more expensive housing and higher living costs, or higher travel expenses for commuters. It is precisely the workers who benefit the most from the metropolitan environment, who are prepared to pay the most to be able to live in a city. Although for businesses in certain regions higher productivity can be realised, that does not result in more profit since labour costs and the price of business real estate are higher. Here too, the businesses that profit the most from the city will be prepared to pay the most for these location benefits.

REGIONAL WAGE DIFFERENCES IN THE NETHERLANDS

A great many studies into regional wage differences and agglomeration effects are conducted with aggregated data. This has the drawback that the regional differences in the composition of the working population are ignored. Since the higher educated prefer to settle in areas with a high economic density and because they earn more anyway, a simple regression of the average wage on the economic density almost automatically leads to a positive correlation. Regressions with data on an aggregated level, therefore, result in an overestimate of the benefits of agglomeration. The use of detailed micro-data about workers, and a two-step approach, can bypass this problem. In the first step it is determined which part of the wage difference is explained by worker characteristics such as age, gender and education. The part of the wage difference that is not explained by these characteristics is subsequently related to the regional and industry characteristics in the second step. From this, the nature and magnitude of agglomeration effects can be inferred.

Figure 4.1 shows the average wage per region in 2005. The wage is standardised so that the average wage throughout the Netherlands equals 100. The average wage is determined per COROP region. The highest wages are paid in Eindhoven, Groningen, The Hague, Amsterdam and other parts of the Randstad area, and the lowest in the northern regions. The high wages in the Zeeuws-Vlaanderen region all have to do with the Dow Chemical Company in Terneuzen.

DUTCH WAGE DIFFERENCES EXPLAINED

Wage regressions are frequently used instruments for the analysis of wage differences. The logarithm of the net hourly wage of each individual is thereby explained on the basis of a constant, the educational level, age and the age squared, and dummies for gender, being an immigrant or not, holding a part-time job as well as the industry and the region where he or she works. The results of this regression analysis are presented in Table 4.2.

A regression coefficient of 0.01 means that when an explanatory variable increases by one unit, the hourly wage earned increases by 1 per cent. Therefore, in 2005 women earned 12 per cent less than men, immigrants 10 per cent less than non-immigrants, and part-time employees 11 per cent less than their full-time colleagues, and all this with otherwise equal characteristics. Workers who completed university studies earned approximately two-thirds more than those who only finished primary school.

Although the individual characteristics explain the wage difference to a great extent, an important part remains unexplained. The question is to what degree this unexplained part can be attributed to regional wage differences. Figure 4.2 shows the wage differences between the regions after correction for the differences in personal characteristics on the basis of the results in Table 4.2. For the most part, the regional pattern corresponds to the pattern in the average wages (see Figure 4.1) but the differences are far smaller. In Figure 4.1, the difference between the highest and lowest wage was 20 per cent; in Figure 4.2 it was only 10 per cent. We may conclude

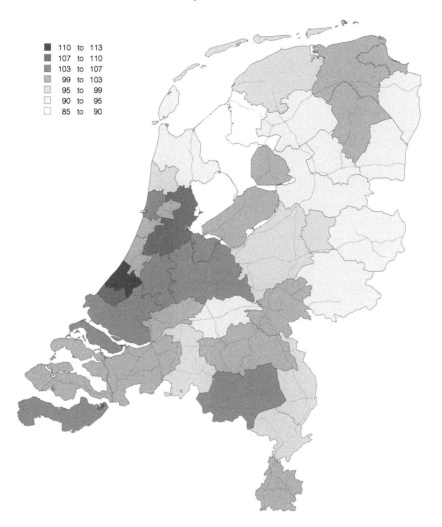

■	110 to	113
■	107 to	110
▨	103 to	107
▧	99 to	103
▨	95 to	99
☐	90 to	95
☐	85 to	90

Source: Own processing of data supplied by CBS Statistics Netherlands.

*Figure 4.1   Average wage per region strongly varies (indices, average is
100, year 2005)*

that an important part of the regional wage differences follows from the
regional differences in the educational level. However, that is not the
whole story. Were a random worker to be relocated from the rural province of Friesland to Amsterdam, this worker would be expected to earn
over 10 per cent more.

Table 4.2   Wage differences and personal characteristics in 2005

Dependent variable: log hourly wage	
Age	0.06
Age squared	−0.0006
Female gender	−0.12
Immigrant	−0.10
Part-time worker	−0.11
Educational level dummies	
Lower secondary education (pre-vocational; vocational at level 1)	0.06
Higher secondary education (higher general; pre-university)	0.26
Lower tertiary education (vocational at level 2 and 3)	0.19
Lower tertiary education (vocational at level 4)	0.27
Higher tertiary education (bachelor's degree)	0.47
Higher tertiary education (master's degree; Ph.D.)	0.68
Explained variance	56%

Notes:
The educational dummies are set off against workers with only primary education. All
effects are significant at a 1% level. Region and industry dummies were incorporated.

AGGLOMERATION EFFECTS AS AN EXPLANATION FOR WAGE DIFFERENCES

What is the explanation for the regional wage differences in Figure 4.2? In
order to find out, we computed the average wage for each combination of
municipality, industry and year, while correcting for personal characteristics. Next, we studied how this average wage correlates with urbanisation,
the specialisation in industries, the diversity and the degree of competition
within an industry. Indicators have been developed for all these factors.
Urbanisation is measured by the density of employment and the areal
size of the region. For MA externalities – knowledge spillover within
industries – the presence of the relevant industry in the region is included.
For Jane Jacobs' diversity, Shannon's entropy is taken as a standard for
diversity. A high value corresponds to a great regional diversity in the
industry structure.

   Table 4.3 contains the results of the analyses we performed. A rise of
10 per cent in the density of employment in a municipality corresponds
to a 0.21 per cent higher wage. With equal density of employment, a
municipality with 10 per cent more land has 0.11 per cent higher wages. In
other words, the productivity difference between two regions with equal

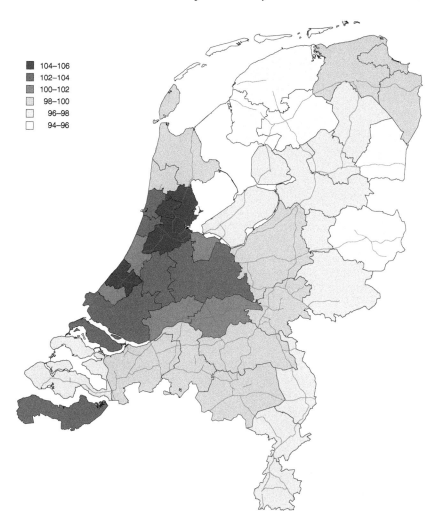

Notes:
Pictured here is an index of the regional average wage residual that remains after correction for personal characteristics. The index is 100 in the region where the wage residual equals 0.

Source: Own processing of data supplied by CBS Statistics Netherlands.

Figure 4.2   Wages after correction for personal characteristics are high in the Randstad area

Table 4.3   Agglomeration effects explain part of the wage difference

	COROP regions	Municipalities
Urbanisation		
Employment density	0.038	0.021
Magnitude (log land surface)	0.013	0.011
Agglomeration		
Industry's presence – MAR	0.024	0.023
Diversity – Jacobs	−0.078	−0.042
Competition – Porter	−0.068	−0.012
Explained variance	32%	19%
Number of observations	7.747	28.048

Notes:
With the exception of competition, all effects for municipalities are statistically significant at a level of 1 per cent. In all cases, industry and year dummies have been incorporated in the analysis.

density is greater for the larger region. These two effects together describe the effect of urbanisation. A strong effect can also be found for the specialisation of a region in a specific industry. Workers in a region where a relatively higher number of colleagues work in the same industry earn a higher wage. A 10 per cent higher presence of the industry goes together with a 0.23 per cent higher wage. Industrial diversity and competition turn out to have a negative effect on regional wages, contrary to the Jacobs and Porter hypotheses.

The practical meaning of the estimated results is reflected in Table 4.4. For each MA, the wage difference vis-à-vis the non-metropolitan areas was determined in terms of percentage. The first column shows the actual wage difference, the second the wage difference as predicted by the estimated model as included in Table 4.3. Although the correlation between the actual and predicted wage difference is strong, for the large cities – particularly those in the Randstad area – a considerable difference remains to be explained; in particular The Hague and Amsterdam stand out. This may follow from the fact that, in case of high urbanisation, the effect on wages increases more than proportionally. It may also indicate that the agglomeration effects of cities in the direct vicinity have, wrongly, not been included in the analysis, while they are especially important in the Randstad area. Finally, they could be the result of a non-observed heterogeneity in individual characteristics, for instance if the best workers within the group of the higher educated take up residence in the largest cities. The

Table 4.4 *Breakdown of the wage difference per metropolitan area (MA) vis-à-vis the wages in non-MA areas, in percentages*

Averages per MA	Observed wage difference	Predicted wage difference	Breakdown of the expected wage difference in the contributions of different components									
			Gender	Immigrant	Part-time	Age	Education	Urbanisation	Diversity	Industry	Competition	Specialisation
Amersfoort	9.88	7.95	0.16	-0.11	0.30	0.56	3.91	2.67	0.10	-0.28	0.65	0.03
Amsterdam	19.52	11.03	0.76	-0.72	0.81	0.41	4.75	5.19	0.04	0.06	-0.27	0.02
Apeldoorn	5.61	3.29	0.50	0.11	0.39	-0.03	0.05	1.87	-0.40	1.07	-0.28	-0.22
Arnhem	6.61	7.46	0.14	-0.03	-0.04	1.46	2.21	3.16	0.27	0.09	0.21	0.10
Breda	2.90	4.01	-0.17	-0.13	0.29	-0.10	1.65	2.82	-0.40	0.43	-0.37	-0.21
Dordrecht	0.63	1.84	0.14	-0.13	0.18	0.15	-0.78	1.64	-0.18	0.57	0.24	-0.16
Eindhoven	8.57	7.35	0.54	-0.23	0.70	0.12	3.59	3.28	-0.23	-0.24	-0.21	-0.19
Enschede	0.15	3.00	-0.02	-0.24	0.03	-0.10	1.71	2.20	-0.38	-0.05	-0.16	-0.11
Geleen/Sittard	4.52	5.33	0.94	-0.05	0.55	2.18	-0.54	1.79	-0.59	0.35	0.71	-0.29
Groningen	7.02	7.78	0.13	0.08	-0.23	-0.42	3.88	3.40	0.24	-0.06	0.77	0.19
Haarlem	7.71	5.58	-0.37	-0.22	-0.09	0.83	2.15	3.07	0.17	0.20	-0.15	0.12
Heerlen	0.17	3.68	0.48	0.00	0.56	1.24	-0.37	1.77	0.01	-0.19	0.18	-0.11
Leeuwarden	0.11	5.02	-0.04	0.19	-0.35	-0.17	1.79	2.66	-0.20	1.40	-0.27	-0.07
Leiden	9.04	5.63	-0.67	-0.28	-0.54	-0.51	3.94	2.36	0.48	0.30	0.56	0.36
Maastricht	4.60	4.20	-0.11	-0.01	0.02	-0.47	2.45	3.10	-0.15	-0.60	-0.04	-0.07
Nijmegen	12.99	8.95	-0.11	-0.16	-0.30	0.80	5.25	3.65	0.38	-0.22	-0.35	0.23
Rotterdam	9.77	5.60	0.30	-0.70	0.63	0.02	1.21	4.23	-0.12	0.25	-0.22	-0.17
's-Hertogenbosch	6.61	5.81	0.32	-0.02	0.39	0.44	2.05	2.75	-0.10	0.22	-0.25	-0.10
The Hague	19.22	11.30	0.47	-0.76	0.98	0.15	4.95	4.68	0.56	0.52	-0.25	0.30
Tilburg	0.81	1.59	0.08	-0.10	-0.10	-1.13	1.01	2.93	-0.03	-0.77	-0.29	-0.15
Utrecht	14.10	10.69	0.53	-0.27	0.42	-0.09	5.30	4.40	-0.10	0.63	-0.14	-0.11
Zwolle	0.63	2.89	-0.02	0.09	-0.31	0.16	0.95	2.62	0.05	-0.42	-0.23	0.19

Notes:
The expected wage differences in percentages are based on the results in Table 4.2 and 4.3.

estimated effect of agglomeration effects, for example, becomes smaller when they are determined by comparing the hourly wage of identical workers before and after a move from one region to another. By looking at relocations, the non-observed individual characteristics are also held constant. The results in Tables 4.3 and 4.4 are in any case consistent with what is known from meta-analyses: the better the corrections for personal characteristics, the smaller the agglomeration effects.

Next, the wage difference between each MA and the non-MA areas was split up into components. The wages are, on average, approximately 7 per cent higher within MAs than outside. Approximately half of the wage differences between MAs and non-MA areas can be explained, the other half cannot. Educational level is responsible for half of the explained part. Only in the seaport city of Rotterdam, the old mining cities of Geleen/ Sittard and Heerlen and in Dordrecht and Apeldoorn does the educational level contribute far less to the explanation of the wage difference. For all MAs, urbanisation clarifies roughly half of the explained part. Apart from education and urbanisations, other factors are of secondary importance. Only in Geleen/Sittard and Heerlen is a substantial part of the wage difference explained by the age structure. The ageing of this region is thus reflected in relatively high wages. In addition, wages in the large cities are held down by the high number of immigrants.

THE WAGE SURPLUS VERSUS THE LAND VALUE SURPLUS OWING TO URBANISATION

The regional differences in wages and land prices show that the Netherlands in an economic sense is far from flat. Productivity is substantially higher in urban areas, due to agglomeration and urbanisation effects as well as a concentration of higher-educated people in urban areas. The monocentric city model of a CBD surrounded by residential neighbourhoods and suburbs predicts that a relationship exists between the net present value (NPV) of the surplus in an urban agglomeration and the surrounding countryside, on the one hand, and the land value surplus in that agglomeration, on the other hand. If the location benefits of the city are the result of higher wages and if all jobs are concentrated in the CBD, the NPV of the wage surplus should be three times as high as the land value surplus. If the jobs are more evenly distributed over the city, the NPV of the wage surplus should still be at least as high as the land value surplus. If not only the jobs in the city are more widely dispersed than the CBD, but also other location benefits contribute to the land value difference between the city and the countryside as well, only then

Table 4.5   Wage and land price differences summarised

MA	Wage premium owing to urbanisation (%)	Wage premium excl. personal characteristics (%)	Built-on land surface (in hectares)	Land price (euro per m²)	Land price difference vis-à-vis non-MA areas (euro per m²)
Amersfoort	2.7	7.7	2112	237	106
Amsterdam	5.2	18.7	7748	717	587
Apeldoorn	1.9	6.5	2305	152	21
Arnhem	3.2	6.0	1773	191	61
Breda	2.8	4.2	2246	234	103
Dordrecht	1.6	2.7	2749	204	73
Eindhoven	3.3	7.1	4967	205	74
Enschede	2.2	1.0	1996	116	−14
Geleen/Sittard	1.8	3.2	2596	101	−29
Groningen	3.4	7.0	2306	241	111
Haarlem	3.1	8.5	2150	493	362
Heerlen	1.8	0.0	3388	91	−39
Leeuwarden	2.7	1.3	1132	184	53
Leiden	2.4	9.5	2432	450	319
Maastricht	3.1	5.8	1489	262	131
Nijmegen	3.6	11.2	1959	208	77
Rotterdam	4.2	12.5	8338	273	142
's-Hertogenbosch	2.8	6.2	2180	308	177
The Hague	4.7	18.1	5261	466	336
Tilburg	2.9	4.0	2802	205	74
Utrecht	4.4	12.6	3852	325	194
Zwolle	2.6	2.4	1423	273	143
Non-MA	0.0	0.0	160 132	131	0

Notes:
The land prices have been determined for the period 2000–2005, prices of 2005.

is the NPV of the wage surplus able to fall below the land value surplus. In determining the land value surplus, it is of course important to know which city boundaries are used. The monocentric city model provides a clear criterion for these: commuter flows. The urban agglomeration is as big as the area from where a significant part of the workers find their way to their work in the city centre.

Table 4.5 summarises the insights into regional differences in land prices and wages that we have gained so far. The first two columns show the contribution of urbanisation to wage differences. The first column exclusively looks at the degree to which wages are higher as a result of the differences in urbanisation (see Table 4.4). The second column represents the total wage difference that has only been corrected for difference in the composition of the population in terms of age, education, gender, ethnic background and full-time employment or not (see Table 4.4.). The last three columns show the built-up surface and land prices (in absolute values and in deviation from the non-MA areas). The land prices here have been established for the period 2000–2005 and are expressed in 2005 prices. The period studied here is shorter than the period on which the analysis in Chapter 2 is based; the land prices determined in that chapter applied to the period 1985–2007. The land prices here are, therefore, more comparable to the wages that also apply to 2000–2005. They were, moreover, less sensitive to the major land price rises that occurred during 1985–2007 (see Figure 2.8). There is, incidentally, a strong correlation between the land prices determined for both periods. The total value of land with a residential purpose can be worked out to be approximately EUR 420 billion. This amount is probably still an underestimate of the true land value, as apartments were not included in the land price analysis, so that the land price in areas with a greater building height is probably underrated. This amount is a net present value. In its study 'Economic effects of regulation and subsidising the rented housing market' ('Economische effecten van regulering and subsidiëring van de huurwoningmarkt'), the CPB Netherlands Bureau for Economic Policy Analysis applied a 5.5 per cent real discount rate for dwellings; included in this discount rate is a 1 per cent relative price rise of dwellings in comparison to the rest of the economy. The return of 5.5 per cent, therefore, comprises 4.5 per cent real net income and a 1 per cent relative price rise. For comparison with the wage surplus, only this 4.5 per cent is important. On the basis of this return, and taking into account the underestimate of the land value surplus, this corresponds to an annual return of at least EUR 20 billion, or more than 4 per cent of the GDP.

The land value surplus of MAs vis-à-vis non-MA areas is at least EUR 120 billion, which amounts to an annual return of EUR 5 billion (see Table 4.6). Irrespective of the previously mentioned reasons for underestimation, for another reason this amount is also an underestimate of the total land value surplus due to agglomeration benefits. After all, the definition of MAs does not fully match the theoretical concept of an urban agglomeration as proffered by the monocentric city model. Whereas the MA definition is based on unbroken building lines, the economic definition is based on the pattern of commuter traffic. The map with commuter flows in Figure 2.7 shows that, from this point of view, agglomerations cover a wider area. The agglomeration of Amsterdam covers the entire area in the Hoorn–Castricum–Zandvoort–Warmond–Hilversum–Almere hexagon, and the Groningen agglomeration also covers its entire province and parts of Drenthe. This difference in the delineation of city agglomerations and

Table 4.6 Wage surplus and land value surplus

MA	NPV of wage surplus owing to urbanisation (billion euro)	NPV of wage surplus excluding personal characteristics (billion euro)	Land value surplus (billion euro)	Land value surplus/wage surplus (column 3/1)	Jobs in MA/ workers living in MA
Amersfoort	1.2	3.5	2.2	1.8	1.2
Amsterdam	16.7	60.2	45.4	2.7	1.3
Apeldoorn	0.8	2.8	0.5	0.6	1.2
Arnhem	1.5	2.9	1.1	0.7	1.4
Breda	1.3	1.9	2.3	1.8	1.2
Dordrecht	0.9	1.5	2.0	2.2	1.0
Eindhoven	3.3	7.1	3.7	1.1	1.3
Enschede	0.8	0.4	−0.3	−0.3	1.1
Geleen/Sittard	0.6	1.1	−0.8	−1.3	1.1
Groningen	2.2	4.5	2.6	1.2	1.3
Haarlem	1.2	3.3	7.8	6.5	0.9
Heerlen	0.8	0.0	−1.3	−1.8	1.0
Leeuwarden	0.9	0.5	0.6	0.7	1.6
Leiden	1.2	5.0	7.8	6.2	0.8
Maastricht	1.1	2.1	2.0	1.8	1.3
Nijmegen	1.7	5.2	1.5	0.9	1.2
Rotterdam	11.0	32.8	11.9	1.1	1.1
's-Hertogenbosch	1.5	3.3	3.9	2.6	1.4
The Hague	8.0	31.1	17.7	2.2	1.2
Tilburg	1.7	2.3	2.1	1.2	1.1
Utrecht	6.6	18.8	7.5	1.1	1.4
Zwolle	1.1	1.0	2.0	1.8	1.6
Total	66.2	191.2	122.0		

the outskirts affects the calculation of the total land value surplus in two ways. First, the size of the urban area is underestimated. Second, the land prices in non-MA areas are overestimated, since the most expensive pieces of land there are unjustly considered to fall outside the MA. One glance at Figure 2.3 shows that EUR 50 per square metre is a reasonable price for the outskirts. For comparison, the price of a square metre of land with a residential purpose in the south-east of the province of Drenthe is about EUR 43, and it is EUR 62 in the Zeeuws-Vlaanderen region.

According to this calculation, the total land value surplus would then amount to at least EUR 305 billion. In order to come up with a picture of the full value of location benefits, the land value surplus of land with a commercial purpose should be taken into account as well. Apart from this land value and assuming an annual return of 4.5 per cent, annual earnings are approximately EUR 15 billion, or around 3 per cent of GDP. It can likewise be determined for each MA how much more is earned than if all workers were to work in the countryside. Thus, a standard is found for the productivity gains resulting from urbanisation: the wage surplus. We based the city's total wage premium on the number of jobs in the MA, taking into account the differences in FTEs and a gross hourly wage of EUR 17.90 for the non-MA area. It makes a difference as to how the wage residual that is not explained by personal characteristics or agglomeration variables is interpreted. A conservative wage surplus standard assumes that the residual is the consequence of the non-observed characteristics of people who cluster in cities. That assumption, therefore, does not allow the wage difference to be attributed to the agglomeration benefit, but rather to the qualifications of the individual. The wage surplus will then amount to approximately EUR 3 billion per year, or approximately 0.5 per cent of GDP. If the residual is fully interpreted as an extra unexplained productivity effect of urbanisation, we arrive at a wage surplus that is three times as high, namely EUR 9 billion per year, or approximately 2 per cent of the GDP. The truth is probably somewhere in the middle.

Be that as it may, even the highest estimate of the total wage surplus is lower than a reasonable estimate of the annual return on the land value surplus. So, the pure monocentric city model, in which all land price differences can be attributed to the higher productivity in the CBD, does not hold. A part of the land price difference must, therefore, be ascribed to local amenities, or the consumer side of the city. The analysis of land prices in the next chapter adds more detail to the impact of these factors.

Between the MAs, there are clear differences in the ratio between land value surplus and wage surplus. It should be noted, though, that MAs such as Leeuwarden and Zwolle have an overabundance of incoming workers commuting between the city and its surroundings on a daily basis. Therefore, the delineation of these MAs' areas is too restrictive, and their land value surplus underestimated. Cities such as Amsterdam, Den Bosch, Leiden and Haarlem have a relatively high land value surplus. In cities such as Rotterdam and Tilburg, it is actually the wage surplus that is dominant. Heerlen and Geleen/Sittard even have a negative land value surplus: the value of their land is lower than in the non-MA areas. The local amenities in these cities, therefore, have a negative rather than a positive effect on land value. The analysis of land prices in the following chapter will shed more light on this.

THE FIVE MOST IMPORTANT CONCLUSIONS

The difference in hourly wages between workers in the Randstad area and the rural areas in the northern and eastern Netherlands is approximately 20%.

In most cities, the percentage of higher-educated people is up to 15% higher than in the non-MA areas. Differences in the educational level explain more than 25% of the wage differences between MAs and non-MA areas.

Urbanisation benefits also explain more than 25% of the wage differences between MAs and non-MA areas. Furthermore, specialisation in industries leads to higher productivity.

The wage surplus of agglomeration and urbanisation is between EUR 3 billion and EUR 10 billion, or 0.5% and 2% of GDP. The total land value surplus boils down to approximately EUR 340 billion (excluding land for commercial purposes), which corresponds to an annual return of EUR 15 billion, or 3% of GDP.

In comparison with the wage surplus, the land value surplus is higher than is to be expected for a monocentric city. It is only in Rotterdam, Tilburg, Heerlen and Geleen/Sittard that the wage surplus is higher.

FURTHER READING

Pierre-Philippe Combes, Gilles Duranton and Laurent Gobillon, 2008, Spatial wage disparities: sorting matters, *Journal of Urban Economics*, 63, 723–42.

Edward Glaeser, Hedi Kallal, Jose Scheinkman and Andrei Shleifer, 1992, Growth in cities, *Journal of Political Economy*, 100, 1126–52.

Henri de Groot, Jacques Poot and Martijn Smit, 2009, Agglomeration, innovation and regional development: theoretical perspectives and meta-analysis, in: R. Capello and P. Nijkamp (eds), *Handbook of Regional Growth and Development Theories*, Edward Elgar Publishing, Cheltenham, UK and Northampton, MA, USA, 256–81.

Patricia Melo, Daniel Graham and Robert Noland, 2009, A meta-analysis of estimates of urban agglomeration externalities, *Regional Science and Urban Economics*, 39, 332–42.

5.   The consumer city

This city is far too beautiful a woman.
De Dijk, 1988

The land underneath the most expensive residential spot in the city centre is more than 200 times as expensive as its cheapest counterpart in the rural areas of the province of Groningen. How is that possible? The previous chapter showed that in the city more money can be earned than outside it. That wage surplus explains a part of the land value surplus, but not all. Apart from the wage that can be earned, the variety of jobs on offer is also important to the value of residential locations. In determining the price that a housing consumer is prepared to pay, the wage level and the (future) career opportunities also carry weight. Particularly since the number of double-income couples is growing, more and more people strategically opt for a place to live where career opportunities are optimal for both partners.

However, the willingness to travel far for work has also increased considerably over recent decades. This is not only due to the substantial improvement in travel speed, but also to the fact that it is often no longer required for people to work from nine to five, five days a week, at their employer's location. The presence of jobs in the city centre, or even in the city, is therefore – and certainly in the Netherlands where cities are closely situated to one another – no longer the only issue. It is the accessibility of jobs from the living location that has become an important consideration. Those jobs may be found in the suburbs, but also other cities.

Since jobs can be reached over increasingly greater distances and many things can be managed and procured through the Internet, the housing consumer has a growing number of potential living locations to choose from. Apart from the quality of the dwelling and its direct surroundings (green and safe), the proximity of urban amenities plays an increasingly greater role in the households' choice of location. The 'new urban residents' want to have these amenities far closer to their homes than their work. They wish to use them on the spur of the moment whenever they like, or at least have the possibility to do so. They are, therefore, less willing to travel for a night out than for work.

Figure 5.1 shows that more than 60 per cent of the working population

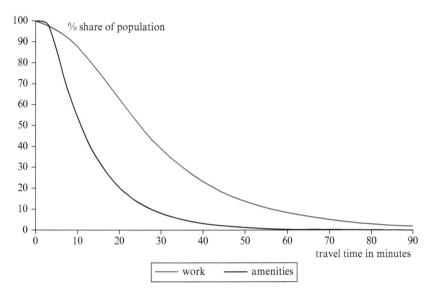

Notes:
The graph shows the part of the working population that is prepared to travel a certain time for work by car.

Source: Atlas voor Gemeenten.

Figure 5.1 *People are prepared to travel longer for work than for urban amenities*

is prepared to travel 20 minutes to work by car, whereas only 20 per cent of the population is willing to do so for a show in the theatre, shopping or a visit to a restaurant. Incidentally, people are prepared to travel a bit longer to and from work when they depend on public transport. For outdoor nature recreation, their readiness to travel is greater than for urban amenities, but less than for work.

Is it this access to jobs or is it the proximity of urban facilities that dictates land prices? In order to investigate this, land prices were related to different environmental characteristics. The environmental characteristics were divided into three categories: work/wage, amenities and disamenities. These are categories of factors that households take into account when choosing their living location. These factors determine the differences in the appeal of potential locations in which to live, and thus the differences in land value.

Gerard Marlet (see further reading) demonstrated in an earlier study that the variance in the location component of house prices in the

Netherlands can, for half of cases, be explained by access to work, and for the other half by city-specific factors. On the basis of the same indicators, we explained the variance in land prices. The expectation was that work/ wage and amenities would positively correlate with land prices (the greater the chance of work and a higher wage, and the more amenities, the greater the demand for a certain living location), and negatively with disamenities (the less safe the surroundings, the less people would be prepared to pay). The results of estimating the model are presented in Table 5.1.

WORK AND PAY

The wage level in a municipality is based on the analysis in the foregoing chapter, where wages were corrected for differences in personal characteristics. That wage level explains part of the differences in land prices. The coefficient is 6.43 – one euro extra pay is associated with 6.43 euro extra land value per square metre.

Another explanation for land prices is the variety of jobs. This does not (only) concern jobs in the direct surroundings of the living location, but (also) the accessibility of jobs within an acceptable travel time. How many jobs can be reached from a certain living location within an acceptable time was determined on the basis of the average willingness to travel for work (Figure 5.1). The access to work per living location was calculated by establishing the travel time from each living location to each work location, both by public transport and by car, taking into account the traffic jams. The number of jobs in the work location was then multiplied by the part of the working population in the living location that is prepared to travel the distance in the associated time. Added up, this resulted in the number of jobs per work location that can be reached within the acceptable travel time.

From the regression analysis followed a coefficient of 0.18 for access to jobs by car. Access to work was expressed in numbers of jobs × 1000. This means that if, from a certain living location, 1000 jobs can be reached within an acceptable travel time, land prices were expected to be EUR 0.18 per square metre higher. Incidentally, more than one million jobs can be reached within the acceptable time from many living locations in the Randstad area. The reduction of traffic jams might just lead to hundreds of thousands of additional jobs and a corresponding rise in land prices.

Access to work by public transport also correlates with land prices, however the effect is smaller (0.09). This access to jobs by public transport was measured at the municipality level. Because of the need for

Table 5.1   Work and amenities each determine around 50 per cent of the variance in land prices

Dependent variable: land prices (per m² at PC-4 level)	Average over the period 1985–2007	Explained variance (without co-variance)	Explained variance (with co-variance)
Gross hourly wage (in €)	6.43	1%	1%
Access to jobs, by car, corrected for traffic jams (× 1000 jobs)	0.18	13%	25%
Access to jobs, by public transport (× 1000 jobs)	0.09	3%	6%
Proximity of railway station	67	1%	2%
Proximity of natural land (access to natural amenities)	0.15	2%	4%
Proximity of city park (surface of park in the neighbourhood)	213	1%	3%
Location at the seaside (neighbourhood by the sea)	75	1%	3%
Historical inner city (number of National Monuments per 100 000 homes in the municipality)	1.70	4%	8%
Location within the Amsterdam ring of canals (0–1 variable)	1.491	0%	0%
Proximity of cultural amenities (access to performing arts)	0.16	4%	7%
Proximity of culinary amenities (access to quality restaurants and bars)	6.63	1%	2%
Proximity of shops for fashion and luxury items (access to shops for 'fun shopping')	0.71	6%	11%
Decline in facilities for daily needs (distance to sufficient shops for all daily shopping)	−7.73	2%	3%
Public nuisance, degeneration, and unsafeness (part of the population that is troubled by public nuisance, degeneration, and unsafeness)	−1.14	1%	2%
Total		41%	77%

Notes:
All variables are statistically significant at the 1 percent significance level. Prices based on the year 2007.

Sources: Land prices: own calculations based on data provided by NVM (Dutch Association of Real Estate Brokers); other data: Municipal Atlas.

transportation before and after reaching a railway station, the proximity of a station is an additional explanation for land prices. The presence of a nearby station leads to a land price that, on average, is EUR 67 per square metre higher than in a neighbourhood without a railway station.

Figures 5.2 and 5.3 show that the contribution of access to jobs to land value is the greatest in the Randstad area. It is striking that for the accessibility of work by car there is a great difference between, on the positive side, the Randstad area (especially the northern wing) as well as – to a lesser degree – the Brabant city triangle of Breda–'s-Hertogenbosch–Eindhoven and the Arnhem–Nijmegen region and, on the negative side, the rest of the country, but that within the Randstad area there is no great difference between living locations in the cities and their surrounding areas. For access to work by public transport, on the other hand, there is a sharp distinction between cities and countryside. The structure of the Dutch railway network is clearly recognisable in Figure 5.3. In the large cities, the effect of access by car and public transport on land prices is approximately equal, whereas outside the cities access by car plays a far greater role. Public transport is a typical large-scale public facility that only has a sufficient economic basis in urbanised areas. However, access to work by public transport cannot fully explain the land value surplus in the city as compared to the surrounding areas. So there must be other factors behind this as well.

AMENITIES

Amenities are all aspects that make a living location a pleasant one, such as a friendly climate and the proximity of nature (natural amenities), as well as urban facilities, such as an attractive historical city centre with culture, restaurants and bars and shops (urban amenities). Disamenities are the negative aspects of a living environment, such as public nuisance, unsafeness, degradation or the decline of the level of facilities for daily needs.

In the analysis, we used unique indicators for amenities that matched, as closely as possible, with the theoretical knowledge about factors that play a role in households' decisions about a home. We did not simply count, for instance, the total number of restaurants, but also took into account their culinary value. Otherwise, as comparable analyses conducted in the United States happened to show, misleading results would emerge – such as a negative correlation between house prices and a restaurant index in which kebab shops carry the same weight as Michelin-starred restaurants.

The indicators we used covered the entire range of potential amenities,

land prices (euro/m²)

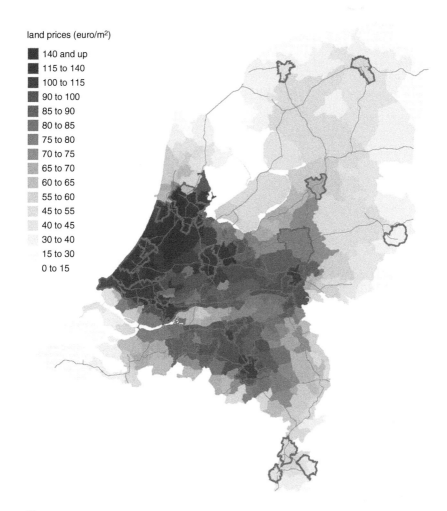

■	140 and up
■	115 to 140
■	100 to 115
■	90 to 100
■	85 to 90
■	80 to 85
■	75 to 80
■	70 to 75
■	65 to 70
■	60 to 65
■	55 to 60
■	45 to 55
■	40 to 45
■	30 to 40
	15 to 30
	0 to 15

Notes:
In black: MA boundaries.

Source: Atlas voor Gemeenten.

Figure 5.2 The better the access to work by car (including correction for traffic jams), the higher the land prices

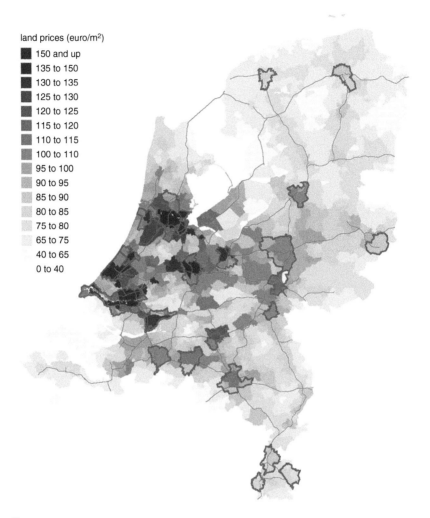

Notes:
In black: MA boundaries.
Presented is the combined effect on land prices of access to work by public transport at
the municipality level and the travel time from a neighbourhood to the closest railway
station.

Source: Atlas voor Gemeenten.

Figure 5.3   The better the access to work by public transport, the higher
*   the land prices*

and not just part of them. This too was done to avoid misleading conclusions. Edward Glaeser, for instance, found a negative correlation between bowling alleys and house prices, but did not include any indicators for unsafeness in his analysis. The bowling alleys in his model thus serve as a proxy for liveability problems. Bowling alleys, after all, often can be found in locations populated by a lower social class where public nuisance and unsafeness also occur the most frequently.

The amenities were measured at different scale levels. We did so because we could not say beforehand whether a certain facility would be primarily appreciated when it was located in the direct living surroundings or whether good access to such facilities in the city centre would be the main consideration. By including the amenities in the analysis at different scale levels and correcting for travel distances, it is not the researcher but the model that determines which facilities at which locations are the most relevant in explaining the appeal of a certain living location, and the price of the land on which it is built.

In particular, the proximity of concert halls and theatres correlates strongly with land price in a living location. The proximity of cultural amenities was measured by counting the number of performances that could be reached from each living location within an acceptable travel time. That calculation was the same as for access to work, but with other travel time values. This indicator for the proximity of cultural amenities explains land prices better than the cultural facilities at the neighbourhood or city level. This means that the cultural amenities in a city increase the average land prices in all neighbourhoods, but mostly in the neighbourhoods from which those amenities can best be reached. The coefficient of 0.16 means that 100 extra concerts or theatre shows (per year) reachable from the home within an acceptable travel time, lead to an average of an extra land value of EUR 16 per square metre in that living location.

Figure 5.4 shows how differences in the cultural amenities correlate with the variance in land prices in the Netherlands. The greatest impact unmistakeably can be found in Amsterdam city centre. Other cities also clearly stand out from their surrounding areas in this, far more than where access to work is concerned.

Likewise, the proximity of shops for fashion and luxury articles as well as quality restaurants was calculated. Having these facilities in the neighbourhood also increases the land value in a residential location. The interpretation of the coefficients was the same as for the cultural amenities.

The presence of a historical inner city (measured by the number of national monuments) offers an additional explanation for the land prices. That history was included in the analysis at the municipality level (not as 'the proximity of'). The interpretation then was that 100 extra monument

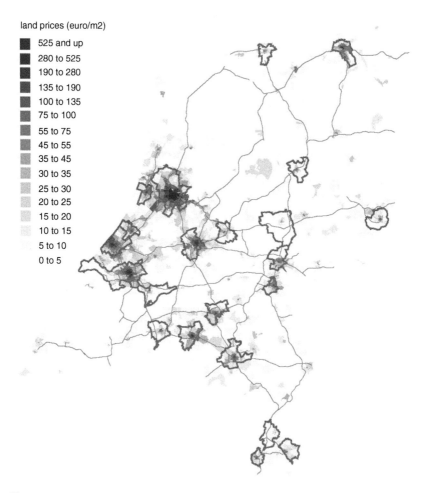

Notes:
In black: MA boundaries.

Source: Atlas voor Gemeenten.

Figure 5.4   Contribution of concerts and theatres concentrates in cities

buildings in a city with 100 000 buildings increases the land value in all that city's residential locations by an average of EUR 1.70 per square metre. A location within the Amsterdam ring of canals even rendered an extra bonus of almost EUR 1500 per square metre of land.

The proximity of natural amenities also results in higher land prices. Apart from a city park in the neighbourhood, people in the cities also want to have nature at an acceptable distance from their homes. The proximity of natural amenities was calculated in the same way as for cultural amenities, although now using hectares and weighted according to the type of 'nature' (forest, water, pastures, etc.). The subsequent interpretation was that 100 extra hectares of nature within an acceptable travelling time from the residential location make the land in that location an average of EUR 15 per square metre more expensive. On top of that, land in neighbourhoods that border on the North Sea coast is, on average, approximately EUR 75 per square metre more expensive than land that is located more inland.

Still to be discussed are the disamenities that decrease the value of land. The relevant explanatory disamenities come into two categories: public nuisance, degradation, and unsafeness on the one hand; the declining level of facilities on the other hand. Public nuisance, degradation and unsafeness formed a combined index of ten relevant indicators, which were expressed in the part of the population in the neighbourhood that is troubled by those problems. That indicator correlated with lower land prices; if 1 per cent of the population in a neighbourhood found their quality of life more than averagely affected by such problems, the land prices were an average of EUR 1.14 per square metre lower. The total explanatory power of this indicator is lower than might be expected. This may be due to the fact that the method described in Chapter 2 could not ascertain the land value in neighbourhoods with only high-rise blocks – which are frequently also problem neighbourhoods – so they fell outside the analysis.

Finally, the decline in facilities was measured as the distance that people have to travel from their home in order to do their daily shopping; the greater that distance is, the greater the decline in facilities. If the distance to daily shopping – due to, for instance, the closing of a bakery in the neighbourhood – increases by one kilometre, the neighbourhood loses an average of EUR 7.73 per square metre of land.

Table 5.1 also presents the contributions of the different factors to the explanation of the variance in land prices. In the first column, we merely looked at the contribution of the individual variables independent of the other factors; in the second column we also took the relations with other factors into account. If all factors are independent of one another in a statistical sense, these two columns are identical. If all factors correlated perfectly with one another, the number in the second column is twice as high as the number in the first column. The latter applies almost everywhere. That agrees with the theoretical expectations. If there is an economic basis for a certain facility in a certain location, there is also a basis for various other facilities at the same time, irrespective of whether these are theatres or a head office with many jobs. Cities are, therefore, places where numerous facilities cluster, and for a very understandable reason.

The calculated contribution of the different factors also offered the possibility to break them down in wider clusters of factors. The product side (wage, accessibility by car, or by public transport with a nearby station) explains 34 per cent of the explained variance of 77 per cent. Amenities (cultural and culinary amenities, luxury and daily shops) explain 22 per cent of the explained variance, and location (proximity of nature, parks and sea, monuments) explains 18 per cent. So the consumer factors together explain 40 per cent. On the whole, the production and consumer sides contribute more or less equally to the explanation for land price differences. Within the city, the consumer side dominates, as the production side is more widely distributed over the cities and their nearby surrounding areas. This especially applies to access to jobs by car.

Other environmental characteristics were also included in the analysis, which did not have a statistically significant correlation with the land price differences. The most striking is the insignificant presence of a university, which in the earlier analysis of house prices did offer an important explanation for the price of the location, and, according to Edward Glaeser, is even the dominant factor in the success of a city in the USA. Libraries, cinemas, cafes, sports facilities and secondary schools offered no substantial explanation for the land price differences between locations either. That might be due to the fact that such basic facilities are present in all cities and are, therefore, not specific to a certain location. The presence and quality of hospitals were not included in the analysis, since a suitable indicator for care facilities is still being developed.

IMPLICATIONS FOR METROPOLITAN AREAS

The implications of these results for the Dutch metropolitan areas (MAs) are presented in Table 5.2 and Figure 5.5. For each MA, the table shows the differences in land prices compared to the non-MA area, both the actual difference (column 2) and the difference as predicted by the model (column 3). For most MAs, the actual and predicted differences are strongly similar. The most important exception is Leeuwarden, for which

Table 5.2   *Breakdown of the differences in land prices in 22 MAs vis-à-vis non-MAs (in %)*

MA	Actual land price difference	Expected land price difference	Wage	Access to work		Urban Amenities				Natural Amenities	Disamenities
				By car	By public transport	Historical city centre	Available performing arts	Available culinary amenities	Available shops (fashion and luxury)	City park, nature, sea	Decline, degradation, public nuisance, unsafeness
Amersfoort	89	94	5	21	29	-2	8	2	16	16	-1
Amsterdam	396	379	12	58	38	49	119	19	80	4	0
Apeldoorn	16	26	5	9	13	-6	0	-2	4	12	-9
Arnhem	41	101	3	28	21	-3	21	-6	27	16	-7
Breda	79	60	2	14	14	-1	10	-2	28	1	-7
Dordrecht	55	68	3	29	23	1	5	-6	12	2	-1
Eindhoven	56	66	3	23	13	-7	14	-1	22	3	-3
Enschede	-9	-21	0	-20	1	-7	10	-5	12	-1	-10
Geleen/Sittard	-24	-26	2	-13	-1	-3	0	-5	10	-9	-6
Groningen	81	48	4	-11	1	1	34	-1	24	-6	2
Haarlem	255	193	3	36	27	8	32	8	44	23	11
Heerlen	-34	-24	-1	-18	-4	-4	4	-6	12	6	-13
Leeuwarden	42	-11	0	-17	-3	6	10	-5	15	-11	-4
Leiden	237	135	6	37	28	4	16	0	29	12	3
Maastricht	86	60	3	-16	-3	25	13	13	38	-3	-10
Nijmegen	44	61	7	23	14	-5	19	-2	20	-3	-11
Rotterdam	101	139	6	29	34	-7	30	3	44	6	-4
's-Hertogenbosch	110	86	4	24	23	0	18	-1	23	-4	-2
The Hague	254	237	11	48	43	-3	45	12	60	16	6
Tilburg	56	71	1	18	18	-6	33	-4	26	2	-16
Utrecht	169	181	6	44	39	1	44	4	42	12	-10
Zwolle	100	37	1	2	11	1	9	1	11	10	-11

Notes:
The expected differences are expressed in percentages of deviation from the average for the non-MA area.

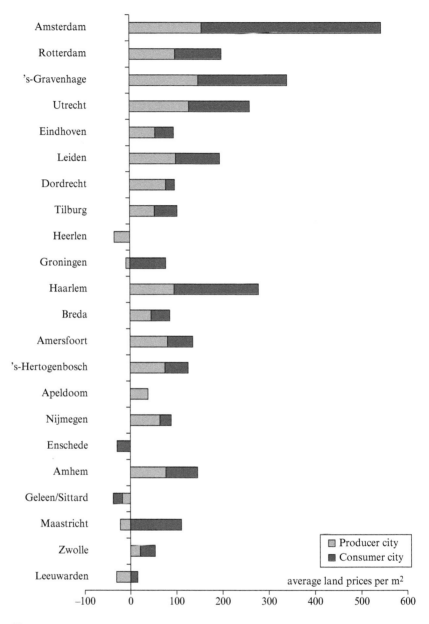

Notes:
Combined contribution to land prices at the MA level.

Source: Atlas voor Gemeenten.

Figure 5.5   Production or consumer city?

the model predicts a land price lower than the price in the non-MA areas, whereas the actual land price there is in fact substantially higher. The differences for Zwolle were also considerably underestimated.

For each of the components of the predicted land price, the contribution to the difference in percentages with the rest of the Netherlands is shown. In the MAs, the land prices are generally considerably higher than in the non-MA areas; in Amsterdam, even almost 400 per cent higher. Only in some (former) industrial cities in the peripheral areas of the country – Enschede, Heerlen and Geleen/Sittard – are the land prices lower than in the non-MA areas.

The wage level and especially also access to work (variety of jobs) offer an important explanation for the high land prices in the cities within the Randstad area. These economic opportunities explain approximately 25 per cent of the higher land prices in Amsterdam. In Utrecht and Rotterdam, these 'production factors' are responsible for approximately 50 per cent of the higher land prices (see Figure 5.5). Amsterdam largely has the available amenities, especially the cultural ones, to thank for its higher land prices. Groningen and Maastricht are also true consumer cities. Apart from its historical city centre and its cultural amenities, Maastricht's culinary amenities also offer a noticeable explanation for its relatively high land prices.

These conclusions closely match the conclusions drawn from the comparison of the wage surplus and the land value surplus drawn in the previous chapter. Compared to their wage surplus, cities such as Amsterdam, Den Bosch, Leiden and Haarlem have a relatively high land value surplus. In cities such as Rotterdam and Tilburg, it is actually the wage surplus that is dominant. Heerlen and Geleen/Sittard even have a negative land value surplus.

Most cities in the Randstad area not only benefit from their great many amenities, but also suffer the consequences of a high level of public nuisance, degradation and unsafeness. In some (former) industrial cities outside the Randstad area – such as Tilburg and Enschede – the decline in the availability of nearby shops for daily needs is an important disamenity. If all those disamenities are combined, Tilburg and Heerlen are the cities where the disadvantages of urbanity have the most negative impact on land prices.

FROM PRODUCER CITY TO CONSUMER CITY

The results show that the city has evolved from a producer city to a consumer city. Urban centres are no longer merely centres for work. Like

Source: Atlas voor Gemeenten.

Figure 5.6   Accessibility of jobs from neighbourhoods in Amsterdam

households, many businesses relocated to the edge of the city in the 1960s
and 1970s. The inner cities changed into consumer centres, with a wide
selection of good shops, restaurants and cultural amenities. Urban centres
may have become more appealing in recent years, but for different reasons
than in the past.

Figures 5.6 and 5.7 illustrate this transition. Access to jobs from
residential locations in the Amsterdam city centre is no better than from
those at the edge of the city, but access to (cultural) amenities is far better
for inhabitants in or around the city centre than elsewhere. Whether the
home is located in or near the city centre is thus more important in terms
of amenities than access to work. Exactly the same mechanism occurs
as in the traditional monocentric city model, only it is not work that is
pivotal, but the amenities. It is all about the choice between a small but
expensive house near these amenities and a larger but cheaper house
further away.

An important reason for this transition is the increasing willingness to
travel far for work and the demand for urban amenities in the proximity
of the home. The little willingness to travel for urban facilities (Figure 5.1)
conversely also means that – contrary to work opportunities – the amenities in a certain city are mainly relevant to the inhabitants of that city

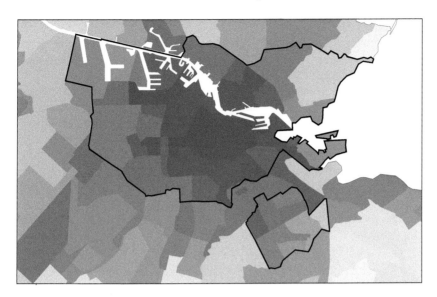

Source: Atlas voor Gemeenten.

*Figure 5.7   Accessibility of cultural amenities from neighbourhoods in
            Amsterdam*

itself. Most performing arts shows take place in the Amsterdam MA, for
instance, which is reflected in its land prices.

THE SOCIAL VALUE OF AMENITIES

On the basis of this analysis, it was possible to calculate the social value
of public goods per city. The value of the total availability of performing
arts in the Netherlands, for instance, amounts to a sum of between thirty
and fifty billion euro, depending on the model used. Assuming an annual
return of 5.5 per cent, this amount corresponds to an annual return of
almost EUR 2 billion. Similar calculations can not only be made for
other environmental characteristics that dictate land prices, but also, for
example, for the value of railway stations and other public transport infrastructure and the social costs of traffic jams.

Such calculations must, however, be used with great care for the time
being. It could be that certain urban amenities that currently matter are
still missing from the model, so that the value of culture is overestimated.
The model presented here will, therefore, have to be further refined, for

example by adding even more types of urban amenities so that the chance is reduced that the impact of a certain amenity also partly encompasses the effect of something else. These land value models will then render a more precise estimate for the value of public goods.

That value is an essential input for the social cost–benefit analyses of government investments in facilities and infrastructure. This calculation applies to existing facilities; it cannot simply be translated into the value of new facilities. After all, the regression analyses are based on actually real-ised facilities. Assuming that these facilities have been realised for good reasons, they will have a greater impact on the land value surplus than a facility that is randomly built in any other location, so that the coefficients found are an upper limit.

The great importance of the clustering of people and businesses has far-reaching consequences for spatial policy. The sensitivity of the land price to environmental factors by definition means that important exter-nal effects occur. Investment in a property by a single owner increases the value of the adjacent plots. Owners, however, do not include this positive external effect on their neighbours' property in their decision to invest and, therefore, they invest less than would be desirable from a social point of view; so the market fails. There is a market for governmental interven-tion and spatial planning to repair this market failure.

THE FIVE MOST IMPORTANT CONCLUSIONS

People want to travel less far for amenities than for their work. The effect of those amenities on land prices is, therefore, far more local than the effect of access to jobs.

77% of the land price differences can be explained by a limited number of factors, such as access to jobs, public nuisance, a historical city centre and amenities such as cultural amenities, shops and restaurants.

Factors on the production side (access to jobs) and consumer amenities each explain about 50% of the land price differences.

The availability of luxury shops, a historical city centre, restaurants and cultural amenities together determine 30% of the land price differences.

The car plays a three to four times bigger role in access to jobs than public trans-port, except in large cities and along some rail routes, where both are equally influential.

FURTHER READING

Terry Clark, 2004, *The City as an Entertainment Machine*, Elsevier, Amsterdam.

Richard Florida, 2002, *The Rise of the Creative Class*, Basic Books, New York.

Edward Glaeser, Jed Kolko and Albert Saiz, 2001, Consumer city, *Journal of Economic Geography*, 1(1), 27–50.

Philip Knapp and Thomas Graves, 1989, On the role of amenities in models of migration and regional development, *Journal of Regional Science*, 29(1), 71–89.

Gerard Marlet, 2009, *De aantrekkelijke stad*, VOC Uitgevers, Nijmegen.

6. Land prices and governmental policy

The reorganisation of public administration is advanced occupational therapy.
Friso De Zeeuw, 2010

One of the figures in the film *The Godfather* is Moe Green. Moe Green is presented to the audience as the imaginary founder of Las Vegas. It was, in the words of one of the Mafia bosses, a visionary idea: it did not involve any spatial planning whatsoever. Moe Green put Las Vegas on the map as a private initiative. He cashed all the profits and used them to further adorn his creation: making the Strip even longer, the Bellagio fountains even more beautiful. All these facilities could be paid for from the land proceeds; no taxes whatsoever were levied. This concept of a city as the project of a single private person seems unreal to the Dutch. Still, it is a useful frame of reference in considering governmental policy where spatial planning is concerned. What goes wrong if a city is taken to be a project of the city's council that develops the city with a view to maximum revenue, but also in competition with other cities that all strive after the favour of potential inhabitants? Land prices are closely linked to the level of the facilities in the direct surroundings. The total surplus value of land for residential purposes in Dutch cities amounts to approximately EUR 340 billion. Topping that is the land value surplus of business dwellings. In other words, there is a great social importance involved in the availability of these facilities. What demands does that place on the organisation of public administration?

The well-being of city dwellers depends on the distance to, and the quality of, the public facilities in their surroundings. An investment in an improvement in that quality, therefore, has a positive effect on their well-being. People are then prepared to give up more purchasing power in order to live close to those facilities: the land value rises. That rise is a measure of the residents' appreciation of the facility's quality improvement. The benefits of the investment in the public good thus capitalise in land prices.

The remarkable thing about this result is that making public facilities locally accessible seems to bypass a problem that exists in the availability of collective goods on a national level. It is generally difficult for governments to determine how much citizens are prepared to pay for collective goods, due to the 'free rider problem': people have a tendency to exaggerate their appreciation for collective goods as long as the community pays for them, and to disguise their appreciation when they have to pay for them themselves. Capitalisation in land prices offers the opportunity, at least for public facilities of a local nature, to ascertain the true appreciation by comparing the land proceeds before and after the investment in the public facility. This unique characteristic of the land market is the motivation for numerous empirical studies into home and land prices.

A consequence of the capitalisation result is that the objective of a well-meaning local government agrees with that of a private city developer who buys all the required land from farmers for a price that is equal to the value in agricultural production and sells it by auction to the highest bidding households after the creation of the public good. The well-meaning local government would invest in the public good until the social benefits (that is to say, the sum of the benefits for all individual users) equal the marginal costs; this is known as Paul Samuelson's Rule (PSR). The private developer invests until the increase in land proceeds following an additional investment equals the marginal costs. Due to capitalisation, however, the social benefits of an additional investment equal this rise in returns.

The profit of a private city developer comprises the difference between the proceeds from auctioned urban land and the costs involved in the buying of agricultural land and the acquisition of the local public good. If the land value surplus exceeds the expenditure for the public good, the developers make a profit, and it is lucrative for an entrant developer to build a new city. This process will continue either until everyone lives in the city and the developers must offer an increasingly more attractive package to draw new residents, or until agricultural land becomes so scarce that the price gradually increases and the locations for new cities become increasingly less attractive. In a market equilibrium, the developer of a new city does not make a profit, as the difference between the total proceeds of urban land and the agricultural land value of this land is equal to the costs of the public good. This is known as the Henry George Theorem (HGT). Private developers, therefore, do not only have the right incentives to offer an optimal selection of public facilities, but also the land market provides them with the necessary resources. So, Moe Green's model is not half as bad as it looks.

PUBLIC FACILITIES OR CLUB GOODS?

In summary, city planners who hold all the land can cover the costs of a public good by the land value surplus. They moreover have the right incentives to construct those public facilities. City planners try to develop these facilities in such a way that the city area yields the most in the ground lease. They therefore build exactly those facilities that yield the most social benefits. It has nevertheless proved difficult in practice to create the situation in which the city's council holds all the land and all the public facilities can be financed from the land value surplus.

Which problems occur when public facilities are not funded from the land rent but, for instance, by entrance fees or membership contributions? Typical examples of facilities that are financed in this way are a swimming pool or a sports club. In the economic literature, such goods are referred to as club goods. Compared to funding from land value surplus, this way of funding has three disadvantages. The bold line in Figure 6.1 represents the course of the land rents in a city with public facilities in the centre without an entrance fee. The land interest close to the public facility is higher, as the city dwellers who want to use that facility have less distance to travel. Just like in Chapter 2, the land value surplus thus equals the benefit of the

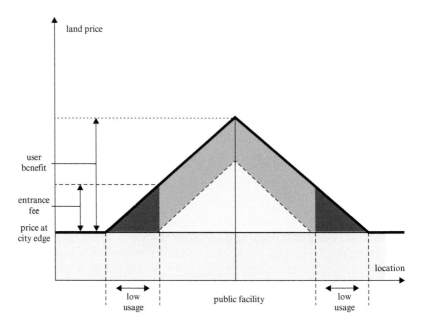

Figure 6.1 Land interest is higher in the proximity of the public facility

use of the public facility less the travel expenses to get there. In the middle of the city centre, the travel expenses are nil, so that the land value surplus equals the user benefit. At the edge of the city, the travel expenses are precisely equal to the user benefit, so the land value surplus is nil. Further away, people simply do not use the public facility.

The dotted line in Figure 6.1 shows the course of the land rent when the public facility is funded from entrance fees. The land rent then declines, until it precisely equals the user benefit less the travel expenses and the entrance fee. The vertical difference between both land rent lines is thus equal to the entrance fee. The consequence is that the limit to the user benefit moves inward: the city becomes smaller, since it is no longer worthwhile for people at the edge of the city to use the public facility. The orange section represents the total proceeds from the sale of entry tickets. The support for the facility becomes smaller and thereby also the chance of it actually being built. The purple triangles express the lost user benefit: locations where the user benefit is greater than the travel costs to the facility, but where residents abandon the idea of using it as they have to pay an entrance fee.

The lower land price in the centre leads to a second disadvantage. Figure 2.4 shows that a strong positive correlation exists between the land price and population density: the high land prices in the city centre result in a higher population density – the houses there have smaller gardens (see Figure 2.5) and more floors. The population density in the proximity of public facilities is, therefore, higher than at the edge of the city, and certainly higher than in the countryside. That is efficient: after all, the locations close to the public facilities are appealing because of the small travelling distance. Therefore, it is recommended to have many people live there so that as many people as possible can benefit from these advantages. It can be demonstrated that when public facilities are fully financed from land rent, this leads to an optimal population density in the city centre. As Figure 6.1 shows, funding from entrance fees results in lower land prices in the centre and so to a lower, inefficient population density in the proximity of the public facilities. This lower population density near a public facility reduces the support for it, and thereby the chance of it being realised.

There is another, third, disadvantage. Not everyone makes equal use of public facilities. Someone who travels by train every day has more interest in living close to the station than someone who does so only once a month. Living close to the station is of more worth to people who travel by train on a daily basis; they are, therefore, prepared to pay higher prices to do so. The consequence is a sorting process: the people who travel by train every day will choose to live closest to the station, whereas those who do so only once a month will live somewhat further away. However, if the daily train passengers have to buy an expensive train ticket every time, living in the vicinity of a station is less attractive to them. They will, therefore, want to pay less for it. In the consideration of the numerous pros and cons of the various living locations, the proximity of the station will then carry insufficient weight. The sorting process of frequent and less frequent train passengers will be distorted. The defective sorting process of frequent and less frequent train passengers thus undermines the support for the station.

This third mechanism can be generalised into an important general conclusion in the spirit of Charles Tiebout and William Fischel (see further reading): the composition of the populations of cities and villages is not homogeneous, and thank goodness for that. Different groups of people need different kinds of amenities, and there is nothing against housing everyone, as much as possible, according to their specific living desires. One loves a garden, another the pub and the third would rather not take more than two steps to travel to work. Each preference has its price, and the willingness to pay that price is determinant in everyone's choice of location. The idea that the populations of each neighbourhood should mirror the Dutch population as a whole undermines the possibility of an adequate array of public facilities.

SHOPS, BARS, AND RAILWAY STATIONS

The analysis of the land prices in Table 5.1 provides an overview of the public facilities whose availability is capitalised in the value of land as amenities. Apart from the classic public facilities such as railway stations, this list also includes activities that are usually not classified as a public good. What about, for instance, shops and bars? The presence of such facilities has considerable effects on the land value surplus. Does this also mean that we should characterise them as public facilities that should ideally be financed from the land value? This happens nowhere in the world, and there must be a reason. After all, if not, it would already have been done a long time ago. But why is it apparently not a good idea? Are there any principles that explain when something should, or should not, be funded from the land value?

The first principle is that of fixed versus variable costs. Public facilities are collective goods; their use has two characteristics: it is (i) non-rival, and (ii) not exclusive. Non-rival means to say that the use of the one does not put restrictions on the use of another. Purely non-rival is the use of television signals: the fact that one person watches channel X is in no way a restriction for another to do so too. Not exclusive means that as soon as a certain facility is realised, citizens cannot be excluded from using it. User fees cannot be charged for such a facility, for everyone is automatically a user. The armed forces are an example: everyone in a country benefits from the protection of its soil. All the facilities discussed here are exclusive. The question is whether their use is rival or not. If it is, there are two possibilities: (1) it has a fixed capacity. In that case there is no distinction between fixed and variable costs. All costs are fixed, and the optimum would be to have the users pay such a high scarcity premium that the demand for the right to use it is exactly equal to the capacity. The remaining costs can best be covered by the land value surplus. (2) The capacity is variable: in that case the optimum would be to request a user fee that is equal to the costs of expanding the capacity. Here, it also applies that the remaining costs would best be covered by the land value surplus.

These rules can be effortlessly applied to railway transport. Suppose that the capacity of the train can be easily expanded, for instance by connecting an extra carriage to the train. According to the above principle, the costs of that extra carriage should be covered by the user fee – in this case, the train ticket. However, the fixed costs of the infrastructure – the stations and the railways – can best be covered by the land value surplus. This leads us to a number of essential characteristics of transport by rail. The railways are an ideal way of bringing large groups of people to one specific spot. Each railway line has extremely high fixed and low variable costs. Therefore, transport by rail is only commercially viable where there are high concentrations of people and only on lines with a high volume, so that the fixed costs can be distributed over a wide group of users. Since these costs are fixed, they can best be paid from the land value surplus. This explains why transport by rail is often publicly provided. The analysis of land prices does not allow for a distinction between railway and bus transport. Out of sheer necessity we have to consider the total land value surplus of public transport (the sum of the factors of access by public transport and the proximity of a railway station: see Table 5.1). This amounts to approximately EUR 90 billion or, assuming a profit of 5.5 per cent, an annual return of approximately EUR 5 billion per year. This is an underestimate of the surplus, since the land value surplus at work locations should also be taken into account. After all, not only home owners pay for the proximity of railway stations, but also employers do. This would roughly lead to twice as high a surplus. For comparison, we could look at the annual public transport subsidies of a total of EUR 4.5 billion (2 billion for city and regional transport, and 2.5 billion for Dutch Rail). This analysis clarifies why transport by rail is primarily financed as a public facility. At the same time, this is an overestimate of the surplus, because the land price effect of the access to work by public transport is a combination of the availability of both work and the public transport infrastructure. Attributing the land value surplus to both underlying factors requires a more detailed spatial analysis.

This first principle of fixed and variable costs still does not answer the pressing question as to why public transport is, and bars and shopping centres are not, funded as a public good, whereas both groups of facilities are capitalised in land prices. The second principle sheds light on this. The manager of the facility must receive sufficient incentives for proper management. The more difficult it is to assess the quality of the management, or the more sensitive the manager is to financial incentives, the stronger the incentives must be and the harder it thus is to compensate the manager from the land value surplus. Pieter Gautier, Michael Svarer and Coen Teulings demonstrated that Copenhagen is Denmark's marriage market, especially for higher-educated people (see further reading). The city is, therefore, not only a meeting place for work, but also for private matters. Restaurants, bars etc. play a key role in this, as that is where people meet. Something similar applies to shops. Bars and shops are in fact fully financed from user fees: the price of a beer or a smart pair of trousers. Yet, the land value surplus shows that they also have the nature of a public good. Why are bars and shopping centres not – partly, at least – financed as such? The first question is whether that doesn't already secretly happen. The properties within a local shopping centre are underhandedly subsidised by putting the properties at the disposal of the shopkeepers for less than the actual costs – this holds in particular for the main crowd-pullers in shopping centres, such as department stores and supermarket chains. This analysis demonstrates why that is a good thing: their function as a crowd-puller turns their presence into a public facility for the other shops. However, pub landlords and shopkeepers, in their turn, are allocated at most a part of the land value surplus which they create in their surroundings by the local city council. Why is that? The reason is that the quality of the facility is very difficult to put down in a contract, so that a strong stimulus is needed in order to make the landlord offer the proper service or the shopkeeper procure a suitable array of goods. The best assessors of landlords and shopkeepers are their customers. The necessity of a strong stimulus undermines the possibilities for public funding. It is relatively easy to draw up contracts for the railways, so that public funding is possible. However, the great many complaints about their customer-friendliness shows that even for transport by rail it is difficult to draw up a conclusive contract, and is it apparently not easy to make the driver and the ticket collector as client-conscious as the shopkeeper on the corner.

The public nature of facilities like bars and shopping centres clearly shows that the decentralisation of public administration can also go too far. The range of the land price effect of such facilities is a good measure for the radius within which the people living in the neighbourhood appreciate their proximity, and thus the scope of public administration. The people in the direct neighbourhood are, after all, often inconvenienced by the proximity of such facilities, due to the noise and the parking problems. If the level of organization of public administration is too low, it places too much weight on the interest of the people in the direct neighbourhood at the expense of those benefiting from a somewhat greater distance. Sub-municipalities are, therefore, for numerous decisions at too low a level. This especially applies to sub-municipalities in city centres, since it is precisely these city centres that provide a basis for wide-reaching facilities while, as sub-municipalities, they tend to not take sufficient account of the interests that are at play across their boundaries.

THE LIMITS TO HGT AND PSR

Many facilities, from railway stations to theatres, from lamp posts to parks are funded as public facilities from collective resources. However, the land value surplus is not the tax basis for the collection of these resources, at least, not in the Netherlands. This is in deviation from the principles of HGT/PSR. The local land taxes play a greater role in the funding of local public facilities in Hong Kong and the United States. Table 6.1 shows that transfers from the state are the primary sources of income for Dutch municipalities. The greater part originates from the General Grant (GG) from the Municipalities Fund, which is paid from the taxes levied mainly over the factor of labour. The inflow into the Municipalities Fund is linked to central government expenditure. The GG for an individual municipality is determined on the basis of a complex formula that is dependent mainly on the size of the population. This does not include the four major cities or the Frisian Islands as their grants are determined in a different way. A similar arrangement applies to the provinces, but they receive a far more modest income than the municipalities. Municipalities often also have the proceeds from land sales and legal fees to depend on. The property tax, where HGT/PSR comes in, forms merely a tiny part of the municipal income. Another two taxes are also based on the value of a property, namely a tax on the imputed income from home ownership and stamp duty. The ground lease system is also a source of income for a number of municipalities. The strange thing is that these taxes would provide wonderful incentives for a local councillor to invest in an optimal package of facilities, according to HGT/PSR. However, these taxes melt into the general resources, and thus do not contribute to positive stimulants for local government. How can these paradoxes be

Table 6.1   Transfers from the state are the primary source of income for Dutch municipalities and provinces

	Billion euro	% Total	% GDP	euro × 1000 per resident
Municipalities				
Grant from Municipalities Fund	17.7	37	3.1	1.1
Special-purpose grants from state	12.9	27	2.3	0.8
social security benefits, sheltered employment	*9.4*	*20*	*1.6*	*0.6*
housing and infrastructure	*3.1*	*6*	*0.5*	*0.2*
Taxes	4.4	9	0.8	0.3
Sales and income from equity	13.2	27	2.3	0.8
Municipalities' total income	48.1	100	8.4	2.9
Provinces				
Grant from provincial fund	1.3	23	0.2	0.1
Special-purpose grants from state	2.2	38	0.4	0.1
Taxes	1.4	24	0.2	0.1
Income from equity	0.9	16	0.2	0.1
Provinces' total income	5.9	100	1.0	0.4

Source: CBS Statistics Netherlands, 2009 figures.

explained? Which problems are obstructing the practical application of HGT/PSR? There are probably a number of factors that play a role here.

First, the application of HGT/PSR is not easy. It requires that the land value surplus amount be determined. In order to do so, two demarcation issues must be solved: (1) at the bottom – what is the value of agricultural land, for only the excess should be taxed; and (2) at the top – what is the value of the buildings, for these have been built at the expense of the owner and that value may not be taxed away. After all, if it is taxed away, a holdup problem arises: owners will become reticent when it comes to investing in buildings, as they fear that the surplus value generated by their investments will disappear through taxes into the pockets of the municipal council. That council may fulfil the ideal picture of the benevolent dictator, but the landowner certainly did not intend to see the return on his or her investments ending up with the municipality. The problems at the bottom are usually not easily solved either. There is usually no such thing as *the* value of agricultural land. At the one side of the city, its boundaries might, for instance, meet those of a neighbouring city, which increases the value of the bordering land. At the other side, the city might meet the coastline. The value of agricultural land is usually a weighted average of

Table 6.2   Tax on the ownership, use or sale of houses and commercial dwellings

	Billion euro	% Total	% GDP	Euro × 1000 per resident
Stamp duty (6%)	2.7	36	0.5	0.2
Tax on imputed income from home ownership (30% tax over 0.55% property value)	1.9	25	0.3	0.1
Property tax	2.9	38	0.5	0.2
Total	7.6	100	1.3	0.5

Source: CBS Statistics Netherlands, 2009 figures.

the value of various adjacent plots. These two demarcation issues cannot be solved just like that. They make property a less efficient tax base than HGT aims for. Including the value of agricultural land weakens the link between the tax base and the facilities realised by the municipal council. By incorporating the buildings, the local government creates the holdup problem that we mentioned before.

Econometric techniques, such as those that we used in this study to determine land prices, make a useful contribution to the solution for both demarcation issues. Various municipalities determine the property tax with the help of similar techniques. Note however that a strict application of the HGT tax would take away all variance in land prices: all surplus value would then be taxed away so that the market value of the land would fall below that of the agricultural land in the surroundings. Table 6.2 provides an overview of the total tax income based on land value. Even if all that income was directly allocated to the municipalities, it would still only comprise 16 per cent of their total income.

There is yet a third, more subtle demarcation issue. As demonstrated by the analysis of Zipf's Law, the development of the land value surplus in a location is also largely determined by coincidence. In the course of the twentieth century, Middelburg and the old Hanse towns lost their importance, whereas the significance of the Brabant city triangle of Breda–'s-Hertogenbosch–Eindhoven grew strongly. Leiden started a protracted decline following the reclamation of the Haarlemmermeer sea. Which cities will be growing in the days to come, and which not, is thus largely based on chance. A part of the value of agricultural land exists in the optional value of building residential dwellings on it later on. As soon as a building has been erected, the difference in value of the land in built-on and vacant states should be equal to the building costs. However, if a location loses its appeal, the value difference will fall below the building costs, for if the landowner had to choose again, they would opt for leaving the land vacant. Since their investment is irreversible, they do not have the possibility to go back on their first decision. The option value of land is a kind of premium for insurance against the risk of the building losing its original value in the future. If that optional value were to be taxed away, it would remove the stimulus for the owner to invest in a building. That makes it even more difficult to distinguish between the value of land and the value of buildings.

The second factor that renders a strict application of HGT/PSR impossible is the course of history. At the moment that an owner of a piece of land is handed a land value surplus on a plate by sheer coincidence – remember the chance factors that underlie Zipf's Law – there is nothing against their pruning away that surplus. After all, it landed in his or her lap – they did not have to do anything for it. To give an example: the fact that a farmer happens to be born near a large city is, all things considered, no reason to allocate the full land value surplus of the future conversion of their fields into new city districts. However, if the government does not respond immediately, the farmer has long since sold the option of converting their land to some project developer. The latter did make an effort to procure the option: they figured out the most likely moment of conversion, how much they would earn from such a conversion and, finally, they paid for it. From the moment the option is sold, the government can no longer prune away the land value surplus, for a new holdup problem would arise since the rights of ownership are no longer certain. In summary, chance profits in land value surplus can only be pruned away at the moment they arise. HGT/PSR are, therefore, partly not applied, simply because the government failed to do so in the past. In that case, mistakes made in the past do offer one guarantee for the future: they cannot be undone just like that.

Last, not all public facilities are realised publicly. The shopkeepers association in a shopping street is a typical example of a private initiative that attunes the interests of the different shopkeepers and so generates a public good. Diversification in shopping centres is an important activity: the right combination of expensive 'look-don't buy' businesses and shops with a more appealing price–quality ratio. This leads to greater external effects: the attractive shop window of the one results in trade for the other. That is why it is easier for shopping streets to flourish when there is some degree of centralisation of property, in one hand or in a limited number of hands. The interests can then be better attuned to one another and the external effects are more easily internalised. Similar arrangements arise around railway stations. It is certainly not without reason that property management is Dutch Rail's moneymaking machine. By erecting office buildings in the direct vicinity of its stations, Dutch Rail manages to prune away part of the land value surplus. This also provides Dutch Rail with the right incentives to furnish its stations as appealingly as possible, and to gear its train schedules optimally to commuter traffic. When a railway station is being renovated, all other owners of properties nearby are also usually asked for their involvement in order to also include the increase in their land value surplus in the renovation. The development of the shopping street and the station are examples of Moe Green at a local scale. If the full land value surplus were pruned away by the government, this would make it impossible for Moe Green to function due to, again, the holdup problem: after the realisation of the project, all benefits will accrue to the government.

In other words, a straight application of HGT/PSR is not easy. However, it is a 'no regret' policy to reform the levying of taxes in such a way that taxes levied on land will be to the benefit of the municipal council under whose jurisdiction it comes, without a redistribution through the municipal fund first. That way, the municipal councils will have the right incentives to maximise their tax basis. Furthermore, the property tax should be reformed so that the full land value will not be taxed, but only the surplus above the value of agricultural land. This implies pleading for the integration of the imputed income from home ownership and stamp duty in a land tax to the benefit of municipalities. This reform of stamp duty would, moreover, have the added advantage that relocation is no longer discouraged at the expense of mobility in the housing market, and so also in the labour market. As PSR shows, such a measure would provide the local government with the best incentives for developing a cost-effective array of public facilities.

SCALE BENEFITS IN A CENTRAL BUSINESS DISTRICT

So far, the fixed costs of public facilities have been the source of agglomeration: in a larger city, these fixed costs can be spread over a greater group of inhabitants. HGT may also be argued for a monocentric city where all workers take up residence around a central business district (CBD). During the production process, businesses and workers develop knowledge. They benefit from each other's acquired expertise. The more production in a city, the more knowledge is gained and exchanged. The productivity of each worker increases in accordance with the size of the city, as revealed by the higher wages and the higher land prices for office locations in larger cities. This agglomeration benefit has the characteristics of an external effect. When a company hires an extra worker, the production scale increases, and so does the knowledge; other companies benefit from this. The company should, therefore, not only reward workers for their contribution to its own production, but also for their contribution to the city-wide knowledge to which they have added. However, companies are small in comparison to the total employment within the CBD. That is why they will ignore the effect on productivity in other companies and only pay for what the workers yield for their own business. The consequence is that there are not enough people working in the CBD, and that the scale of the production process is smaller than would be desirable from a social point of view.

A local government can repair the efficiency of the urban production process by subsidising wages. This subsidy should be high enough to make up the difference between an additional worker's contribution to the total production and to the production of an individual company. After all, such a subsidy would draw a sufficient number of workers to the city in order to reach an efficient scale. However, it appears to be far from simple to actually find out exactly how great the contribution of an additional worker to the city's production is. Knowledge is hard to measure, and quantifying its role in the production process is no easy matter either.

Esteban Rossi-Hansberg demonstrated that even in this case the land market brings help (see further reading). What are the profits of a one euro subsidy on wages? The subsidy will draw additional workers from elsewhere in the country, and the wage will rise further than that one euro subsidy, since average productivity will increase in accordance with the increased scale. In equilibrium, workers will have to pay so much more for their land or commute so much further from their homes to the CBD that the increase in their well-being as a consequence of the pay rise is annulled. The profits of the wage subsidy are, therefore, also expressed in land prices. In order to reach an optimal scale, the government should subsidise the wages until the rise in the land proceeds due to the extra euro subsidy equals that same euro. This way, it could theoretically pursue an efficient policy without knowing the details of the production process.

In the context of agglomeration benefits in production through the transfer of knowledge it also applies that a private developer would make exactly the same comparative assessment as a local government. Private developers would develop cities until there is no more profit to be made, so the land proceeds and the total wage subsidy should be equal. As long as local governments were able to seize and optimise the land proceeds, they would – again – have the right incentives and financial resources to implement optimal policy.

STATE INTERFERENCE, PROVINCES, AND MUNICIPAL AUTONOMY

Since the government uses the land value surplus only partly as a tax basis for the funding of local public facilities, it needs alternative tax bases and instruments to channel resources to local governments. As shown in Table 6.1, in reality the General Grant (GG) is the main source of income for lower governments. Can the current form of that income flow be understood from the principles of HGT/PSR and from the problems in applying these principles literally?

Large municipalities receive a higher GG per resident than their smaller counterparts, which is clearly shown by Figure 6.2. The horizontal axis reflects the number of inhabitants (in a logarithmic scale), and the vertical

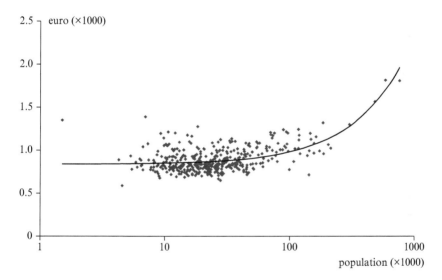

Notes:
2009 figures.
Excluding the four Frisian Islands.

Source: CBS Statistics Netherlands.

Figure 6.2   *The General Grant from the Municipal Fund per resident increases according to the municipality's population*

axis the GG per resident. For municipalities with a population of fewer than 50 000 the amount remains more or less stable: approximately EUR 900 per resident. Above that number, the amount increases up to nearly twice as much for Amsterdam and Rotterdam. How does this correlation between the size of a municipality and the GG per resident fit in with the analysis we discussed above? As we found earlier, the municipalities' ability to utilise the land value surplus as a tax basis is very limited whereas, according to the HGT/RPS principles, it should actually be efficient. Consequently, the Dutch must look for alternative methods for providing the local government of places where many public facilities are being realised with the required resources. Due to the high density, the CBD, or the public facilities, the land value surplus per resident is higher in larger than in smaller municipalities (see Figure 6.1). From this point of view, it is logical that the GG per resident in a municipality with a population of fewer than 50 000 is virtually consistent, as these are rural municipalities or smaller cities where land value surpluses hardly occur. But does the magnitude of the land value surplus justify the higher GG per resident for Amsterdam and Rotterdam? Assuming an average land price of EUR 130 per square metre in the non-MA areas, this surplus amounts to an annual EUR 37.5 billion for Amsterdam and EUR 8 billion for Rotterdam. Based on a profit of 5.5 per cent, this corresponds to an annual return of EUR 2868 per resident for Amsterdam, and EUR 781 for Rotterdam. These amounts are an underestimate of the real surplus, for the value of land for residential purposes in rural areas is significantly lower than the average land price in non-MA areas. On the face of it, in terms of size, the higher GG per resident for large municipalities is quite understandable.

The question now is whether the high GG is the consequence of the high land value, or the other way around – the higher land value is due to the higher GG. Christian Hilber, Teemu Lyytikäinen and Wouter Vermeulen looked into this question for England (see further reading). The Labour government there increased the GG for a number of municipalities, because Labour was in danger of losing the relevant local constituencies. This increase in the GG turned out to be virtually fully capitalised in the land value. Due to the higher GG, the local tax rates could apparently be lowered, and this lower tax burden translated into higher house prices. In other words: the risk of a circular argument is real. However, 77 per cent of the land price differences can be attributed to observable facilities that in many cases are also of a local nature. These land price differences are, therefore, due to the location of the facility in question, and not to a lower tax burden that, as a consequence of the higher GG, applies to the municipality as a whole. The differences in the GG in the Netherlands are not a sound explanation for the effect we found.

The GG is a reasonable substitute for the existing obstructions to applying the HGT/PSR principles in practice. There is, however, one great disadvantage to the financing of the GG from taxes. As Esteban Rossi-Hansberg showed, the optimal financing structure of a city with a CBD is to use the land value surplus for a wage cost subsidy that reflects the positive external effects of an extra worker on the productivity of others. The funding of local public facilities through an income tax does exactly the opposite. The wages in the city are higher than in the country-side, and by taxing that surplus through income tax even more, exactly the reverse is achieved. The scale elasticity of 2.1 per cent in Table 4.3 implies that the marginal productivity of an extra worker is 2.1 per cent higher than average. Take Amsterdam, for example: the wages there (the average productivity) are now approximately 10 per cent higher than for similar workers in the countryside. In terms of marginal productivity, this wage difference should be 10% + 2.1% = 12%, i.e. 20 per cent higher. Figure 6.1 shows that in a one-dimensional city the number of people profiting from this productivity benefit linearly increases with the ascribed benefit. In a two-dimensional city, this number even increases quadratically with the ascribed benefit. This implies that over 40 per cent more people could work in the Amsterdam CBD. Assuming a scale elasticity of 2.1 per cent, this would lead to a productivity increase of around 1 per cent.

Apart from the GG, there are other, specific flows of money from the state to lower governments. Some of these flows are dependent on fixed rules, but for others the size is primarily determined by political decision making, such as the grants awarded by the state for specific infrastructure projects (such as certain grand-scale urban restructuring projects and other spatial planning projects). Insofar as these flows of money depend on fixed formulas between municipalities, one may wonder why these grants are not integrated into the GG. Insofar as these flows of money depend on political decision making at the state level, the question arises of what the optimal level of decision making is. The involvement of one or more higher levels merely leads to a new holdup problem, in which the lower government puts the execution of an otherwise urgent project on hold, simply because they first want to make sure that they will receive funding from the state. This is a first application of the subsidiarity principle: one institution has the authority, or not. If not, it had better not get involved.

THE ROLE OF SPATIAL PLANNING AND ZONING PLANS

There is no greater frustration in the daily life of a private project developer than the zoning plan. It sets out the purpose of a plot of land, in full. May the future building serve as a home, office or hotel? Can it only be used for social-cultural facilities? The latter case would be problematic, for it doesn't pay enough to keep body and soul together. The zoning plan also sets out development boundaries and building heights, and sometimes there are even regulations as regards the required architecture. Zoning plans can be altered, but that is a time-consuming process. It is, moreover, rather the rule than the exception that a municipality sends a hefty invoice for a change in a zoning plan. Whatever the municipality cannot pocket through a tax on the land value surplus, will still be pruned away as much as possible through these invoices. Municipalities moreover manage to prune away a part of the land value surplus by the issue of building plots that they own themselves. Figure 6.3 provides an overview of the amount per resident that municipalities manage to take in through changes in zoning plans. In the 1990s, this amounted to 0.5 per cent of GDP. In recent years, this amount fell rather quickly.

In the simple theoretical world of HGT/PSR, the city planner does not

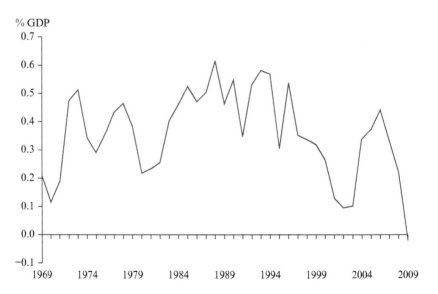

Source: CBS Statistics Netherlands.

Figure 6.3   Net land sales by local government

have a need for the instrument of a zoning plan. A tax on the land value surplus plus a grant for the production factors that contribute to the scale advantages within the CBD would suffice. In that world, there is no designated purpose for a plot and, therefore, the land price is not dependent on that purpose either. There are no such things as a boundary effect whereby the value of the land at one side of a zone with a particular purpose is totally different from that at the other side. As discussed earlier, it turns out that, in reality, HGT/PSR with subsidies for the production factors in the CBD cannot be applied just like that. Esteban Rossi-Hansberg showed that in such situations, zoning plans are a reasonable alternative, for various reasons.

The first reason is that a subsidy on production factors that contribute to the scale advantages in the CBD cannot be realised in practice. The CBD would then become too small, creating an incentive for an inefficient mix of living and working, so that the scale advantages cannot be utilised in full. This trend is counteracted by designating the CBD exclusively as a work location. The consequence is that the land located just within the CBD has a lower price than the land outside it. The lower land price within the CBD is a substitute for the subsidy on production factors on which the scale advantages are based.

A second reason is the user value of public green spaces: public parks and gardens. Jan Rouwendal and Willemijn van der Straaten (see further reading) demonstrated that a public green space has a positive effect on land value over a distance of 500 metres. This externality could be internalised by a grant for the owners of those public green spaces, which is something that already happens through the country estate legislation. A restriction on the purpose that limits the conversion of public green spaces into building land is, again, an excellent alternative. The positive effect on the land value surplus provides an indication for the price difference that can be justified on these grounds. Apart from the benefit to the users in the direct vicinity, there are also wider external effects, such as the maintenance of an unbroken open area. These must be valued separately.

An associated reason for land use restrictions concerns the exact timing of the conversion of public green spaces into a built area and the density that is thereby realised. The local land owners might have an incentive to build in a density that is too low, as they do not take sufficient account of the positive effects of a high density at the edge of the city on the support for public facilities in the centre. Thus, a conflict of interests arises between the landowners in the centre and their counterpart at the edge of the city.

Last, the zoning plan can serve as an alternative for a tax on the land value surplus. The current institutional framework does not allow for the local government to seize the land value surplus in full. For new building projects, municipalities need to negotiate with project developers and other land owners, who all like to pocket their share of the proceeds. The Dutch Spatial Planning Act allows for the costs of local facilities to be recouped to a certain extent, but the municipal council cannot simply recover the costs of facilities in the city centre, such as a theatre, even though these facilities do contribute to the amount of the land proceeds.

LAND VALUE SURPLUS, SUBSIDIARITY, AND THORBECKE'S ARRANGEMENT

According to Friso de Zeeuw, the reorganisation of public administration is advanced occupational therapy. For decades now, the Dutch have been philosophising about a thorough rearrangement of the three levels – the state, provinces and municipalities – that together make up the model that Thorbecke designed for the Netherlands 160 years ago. In the business world, no organisation model is sacred, and new organisational concepts have been launched successfully over the past decades. According to consecutive committees, there is much to be improved in public administration too, but so far it has not led to a great deal of action.

The monocentric model of the city provides insight into the range of the external effects of infrastructure and public facilities. This range stretches as far as the effect of a facility resonates in the local land value surplus. The subsidiarity principle applies here, which was already addressed in the discussion about the financing of major infrastructure projects. This principle entails that political decision making about public facilities must take place at the lowest possible level at which the majority of the external effects of a facility are internalised. The higher the level at which the decision making takes place, the greater are the differences of interest and the holdup problems, and the higher, therefore, the transaction costs involved in arriving at the right decision will be. The monocentric model of the city suggests that most of those external effects do not cross the city's boundaries. These city boundaries often coincide with the municipalities' boundaries. In large urban agglomerations, these external effects have a wider range; the suburban municipalities around the central municipality will also feel their consequences. In most cases, the province does not, a priori, seem to be a logical unit of decision making, since the boundaries of provinces do not coincide with a logical cluster of economic activities. However, the analysis of the land value surplus allows us to abandon this a priori judgement and replace it with an empirically founded assessment. The fact that Chapter 5 revealed that 77 per cent of the differences in land prices can be explained makes for very solid conclusions of such an analysis, as it is unlikely that any important external effects were left aside.

An initial way of gaining insight into the range of the external effects is revealed in Figure 5.1, which shows for each facility how far people are prepared to travel for it. The first thing that stands out is that people are prepared to travel far further for their work than for numerous other facilities. This corresponds to the conclusion that consumer motives carry greater weight in city formation nowadays than production motives. To put it differently: the commuter pattern in the Netherlands today is too varied to still describe it as a simple monocentric city model. This conclusion is confirmed by Figure 2.7, which pictures the commuter traffic in the Netherlands. In this map, for most urban agglomerations the star-shaped pattern of commuter traffic can be recognised, which is characteristic of the monocentric city with a CBD/central municipality that serves as a work location, surrounded by the suburbs/suburban municipalities where those working in the CBD live. Apart from that, however, there are also substantial criss-cross flows between agglomerations that do not follow the logic of the monocentric city. Based on the commuter flows, the greatest urban agglomeration of the Netherlands, Amsterdam, covers the hexagon of Hoorn–Castricum–Zandvoort–Warmond–Hilversum–Almere. The Haarlem MA is, in reality, fully integrated in this area. There exists a considerable commuter flow of people who live in Haarlem and work in Amsterdam. This area covers great parts of the provinces of Noord-Holland and Flevoland, and small parts of Utrecht and Zuid-Holland. This range is, therefore, the upper limit of what may be expected in other urban agglomerations.

Although most of the external effects have a relatively limited range, this range has gradually increased in recent years where the urban agglomerations are concerned. This turned the old municipal boundaries of the cities into a pinching corset within which an increasingly smaller part of the external effects were internalised. Free-riding behaviour arose: suburban municipalities hitched a ride on the facilities of the large city without paying taxes for them. From this perspective, it is not very surprising that the suburban municipalities often felt very little need to merge with a central municipality. Why pay for something that you can get for free? HGT and the levying of taxes based on the land value surplus do, incidentally, offer part of a solution to this problem. As shown by Figure 6.1, the land value surplus at the edge of the urban agglomeration is smaller than in its centre. When tax is levied on the basis of the land value surplus, the suburban municipalities have to contribute less than the central municipality, as the travelling distance to the public facilities is greater. Whereas the contribution of tax to the central facility was the primary consideration for

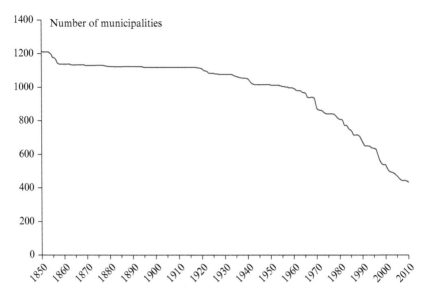

Source: CBS Statistics Netherlands.

*Figure 6.4   The continually decreasing number of municipalities due to
             rearrangements*

some suburban municipalities, the others obstructed the building of new
homes, so that the central municipality could not fully benefit from the
scale advantages in its CBD. Apart from this increased range of external
effects, an adequate public administration required an increasing scale
size, given its strongly expanded and more complex package of tasks due
to the decentralisation of authorities. All these processes together are the
driving force behind the only innovation in Thorbecke's model in the past
century: a continuous process of municipal rearrangement. Figure 6.4
shows how the number of municipalities continually decreased.

The analysis of the range of external effects confirms the conclusions
drawn by earlier committees that Thorbecke's arrangement could do
with a makeover. The distribution of the land value surplus speaks for a
far-reaching decentralisation of spatial planning to the level of municipalities and urban districts. Only in the area of the connections between
the MAs, is a role set aside for the state. At the same time, the centralisation of decision making within the urban districts is needed. Many of the
municipalities within the MAs tend to get in each other's way or at least
reduce each other's strength. As a consequence, the external effects are
not properly internalised within the MA. The question is also whether

---

THE FIVE MOST IMPORTANT CONCLUSIONS

A local city planner who tries to maximise the land value surplus will realise the most socially desirable package of public facilities.

The fixed costs of public facilities must be financed from the land value, and the variable costs from entrance fees.

Financing of the fixed costs of public facilities from entrance fees leads to too narrow a range of facilities, too low a population density in the direct vicinity and too little positive selection of intensive users.

The best way to finance a municipality is through taxes on the land value surplus. The increase in the General Grant from the Municipal Fund (*Algemene Uitkering uit het Gemeentefonds*) per resident according to the size of the population is the second best alternative to a tax on the land value.

Integration of all land-based taxes in one system, and a direct transfer of the proceeds to the local government, improve the quality of this government.

---

sub-municipalities do not have too many authorities. The analysis of the land value surplus does not leave a clear role for provinces. The provincial boundaries rarely, if ever, serve as a useful demarcation of an area within which a considerable part of the spatial external effects are internalised.

FURTHER READING

Richard Arnott and Joseph Stiglitz, 1979, Aggregate land rents, expenditure on public goods and optimal city size, *Quarterly Journal of Economics*, 93(4), 473–500.

William Fischel, 2001, *The Homevoter Hypothesis*, Harvard University Press, Cambridge, MA.

Pieter Gautier, Michael Svarer and Coen Teulings, 2010, Marriage and the city: search frictions and sorting of singles, *Journal of Urban Economics*, 67(2), 206–18.

Christian Hilber, Teemu Lyytikäinen and Wouter Vermeulen, 2010, Capitalization of central government grants into local house prices: panel data evidence from England, *Regional Science and Urban Economics*, 41(4), 394–406.

Esteban Rossi-Hansberg, 2004, Optimal urban land use and zoning, *Review of Economic Dynamics*, 7(1), 69–106.

Jan Rouwendal and Willemijn van der Straaten, 2008, The costs and benefits of providing open space in cities, Tinbergen Institute, Discussion Paper 2008-001/3, Amsterdam-Rotterdam.

7. Agglomeration benefits and spatial planning policy

> What would have happened without a specific overspill policy? Amsterdam
> would have grown into a mammoth city with 1 to 1.5 million inhabitants
> . . . Eventually, the part of the Noord-Holland province around Amsterdam
> would have turned into a car city, something like Los Angeles.
>
> Roel De Wit, 2007

Amsterdam would have grown into a city with millions of inhabitants if the later Prime Minister, Joop den Uyl, had had his way in the 1960s. As the alderman for, amongst other things, urban development and public works, he aspired to large-scale expansion, both by developing land in surrounding municipalities and by drastic restructuring of the historical city centre. In his biography, Annet Bleich (see further reading) referred to a 'Manhattan by the Amstel river'. His appointment as Minister for Economic Affairs in the Cals administration in 1965 put a stop to his plans. Joop den Uyl was succeeded as alderman by Roel de Wit, who focused on Purmerend instead, at that time still a provincial town with about fifteen thousand inhabitants. This was the beginning of the so-called 'overspill policy' or 'growth centre policy', which restricted growth at the fringe of the large cities for the benefit of more distantly located, some-times newly designed, centres of urban growth.

This policy choice to restrict the growth of Amsterdam and other cities in the Randstad area entails both costs and benefits for society. In the quote above, taken from an interview with the *Volkskrant* newspaper, the open space that came through unscathed is emphasised. On the other hand, there is the surplus that households would have enjoyed by living at these locations if land development had been permitted. On top of these kinds of direct effects of spatial planning policy, however, there is an indirect effect. Chapter 4 showed that urban scale leads to benefits, because workers are more productive. Apart from that, the fixed costs of offering certain facilities in a large city can be spread over more households, for instance. If a city is obstructed in its growth, these scale advantages are utilised to a smaller degree: the productivity of workers is smaller and households pay a higher price for some of the facilities, or it is no longer beneficial to provide them. It is this indirect effect that is studied here in more detail. When is it useful to relax spatial planning policy that primarily focuses on direct effects, so that the advantages of agglomeration are better utilised?

A first requirement is that the agglomeration advantages are of an external nature. If individual actors already fully include these advantages in their considerations, or if the government holds a perfect or first-best instrument to internalise them, spatial planning policy does not have to take them into account any longer. In the previous chapter we discussed the example of a monocentric city in which all workers reside around a CBD and where knowledge is developed during the production process. The agglomeration advantage in this example is the fact that more knowledge is at hand in a larger city. Individual companies are, however, too small to take this into account in the remuneration of their employees: the wage corresponds to the average productivity. That is lower than the marginal productivity, since the last employee contributes to the productivity of other workers in the city. Therefore, there is an external effect: in a free market, the city is too small. A wage subsidy could solve this problem, but municipalities rarely use this instrument, as it incurs practical difficulties. The relaxation of spatial planning policy is an alternative way to draw more workers to the city. Instead of wages it is in fact the use of the land that is being subsidised. This chapter revolves around the questions of when it is useful to use this second-best instrument.

When answering this question, we should take into account that a greater Amsterdam would come at the expense of the population numbers elsewhere in the country. It is, after all, possible that other cities in the Randstad area would have stayed smaller, so that the scale advantages would have been used to lesser extent there. From the perspective of society as a whole, this loss in wealth would then, at least partly, cancel out the agglomeration advantage in Amsterdam. Less population growth elsewhere can, however, also be induced by a smaller number of cities. With a less restrictive policy around Amsterdam, growth centres such as Purmerend would perhaps have remained the size of a village, or perhaps not have emerged at all. In that case, other existing cities would not be confronted with a scale loss that would (partly) cancel out the productivity advantage in Amsterdam. The same applies if urban growth occurs at the expense of the number of households in the countryside, where there are, almost by definition, no agglomeration benefits.

PROFIT AND LOSS IN CASE OF A FIXED NUMBER OF CITIES

Suppose that the number of cities in the Randstad area is a given. At first glance, this might seem intuitive, certainly in the short run. The development of a city takes time, and as it requires a minimum scale there must be sufficient demand for it to become beneficial. The government cannot put a new city on the map for 20 home-seeking households. If the overall population declines, the number of cities is also difficult to change, since they are already there. If the required investments have been made already, it would be a waste not to use them. Suppose also that there is no inflow from households from the countryside or from outside the Randstad area (the alternative scenario will be discussed later in this chapter).

What happens when a local government tries to draw an extra worker to its city? The production in this city increases, not only due to what this worker produces herself, but also because other workers in the city become more productive. The first part, the worker's own production, is paid out to her as the wage. The second part is profit for the city. However, if the number of cities and the number of households that must be housed in them are both given, the growth of this city means that another city has to shrink. To a city that loses a worker, exactly the opposite applies. It loses a bit of production and there is one worker less to pay – these effects cancel each other out, but on top of that the productivity of other workers also decreases.

Figure 7.1 illustrates these effects. This figure shows the supply and demand on the labour market in a small and a large city. Companies offer the wage that corresponds to the average productivity of employers, which is higher in a larger city due to agglomeration advantages. The market is in equilibrium if the average productivity equals the wage that workers demand in order to be as well off in this city as elsewhere. In a city with attractive facilities, they do not have to earn as much: the vicinity of a historical city centre or a beach offers compensation. That is why the supply curve of the more attractive city is lower. The more this city grows, the higher the costs rise, as people will have to travel increasingly further to get to work. In equilibrium, the attractive city is larger, and therefore the wages are higher, but the daily life of the households that live there is so much more expensive, that moving there is nevertheless not appealing to the inhabitants of the less attractive city.

The same figure also shows the marginal productivity of a worker. This is the wage that companies should actually be paying in order to internalise the external effect of the transfer of knowledge. If the labour market is in equilibrium, the difference between the marginal and

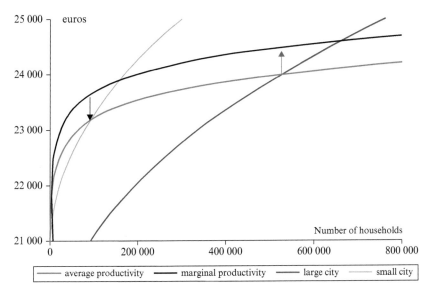

Figure 7.1   Profit in the one city is partly cancelled out by the loss in the other

average productivity corresponds to the profit for the city that manages to draw an additional worker. The arrows in Figure 7.1 represent the profit for the large city and the loss for the small city when a worker moves from the latter to the former. For society as a whole, only the net result counts, which proves to be a lot smaller than the separate arrows. The large city's profit is, therefore, partly cancelled out by the small city's loss.

This is an external effect. If Moe Green, the city developer in the previous chapter, makes Las Vegas grow, he could not care less if a bit of productivity is lost elsewhere. This scenario, therefore, requires policy coordination at a higher level. Optimal exploitation of agglomeration benefits requires cities in which the difference between marginal and average productivity is relatively large to become a bit bigger, and cities in which that difference is relatively small to become a bit smaller. In order to achieve this, spatial planning policy can be used as an instrument. Will that get us anywhere? That depends on the relationship between urban scale and productivity. In Figure 7.1, the difference between the marginal and average productivity only increases very limitedly according to the size of the city, so that profit and loss almost cancel each other out. If the difference between the marginal and average productivity does strongly vary between cities, there is much more to be gained.

A MORE REALISTIC SCENARIO: THE NUMBER OF CITIES ADAPTS

That the number of cities would be an unchangeable given in the long term, is empirically difficult to maintain. Obviously, there are more cities in the Netherlands now than there were a century ago. De Wit's restrictive policy around Amsterdam resulted in new cities in its surroundings: Almere for example. The population may well decline in the future, but households are becoming smaller and urbanisation is still in full swing. The Randstad area, therefore, will face demand for new housing: more houses are needed, and these could be built either in the growth centres or at the edge of existing cities.

In order to create a new city, fixed costs have to be incurred. After all, cities cannot do without a town hall, a police station and other elementary facilities. A developer would build the city if the profit on land would be higher than these fixed costs. Is this efficient? No, not if there is no wage subsidy at hand, for an external effect also comes in to play when a new city is erected. The households that are going to live and work here will be leaving another city, where the productivity will fall as a consequence of scale loss. The creation of new cities will, therefore, have to be tempered.

A higher tier of government can internalise this externality by levying taxes on the creation of new cities. In the Dutch context, in which the central government has been strongly involved in the creation of new cities in the past, this would translate into a little more restraint in the founding of new centres of urban growth. This would result in a smaller number of cities, and the number of households and jobs in each city would be higher. In what respect does this result differ from a first-best equilibrium? A wage subsidy would be higher in cities where the difference between marginal and average productivity is greater, but through a tax on the creation of new cities all existing cities would receive the same push. If great variance exists between the cities in this respect, the loss can be substantial. Once the optimal number of cities has been chosen, is it then still of any use to adapt the spatial planning policy at the edge of the city to the existence of external agglomeration effects? The answer to this question strongly resembles the case of a fixed number of cities: profit in the one city is at the expense of loss in the other, and the net wealth effect is dependent on the relationship between scale and productivity.

Suppose now that it is not possible to levy a tax on the creation of new cities, so that cities keep on appearing and disappearing until the land value surplus of the marginal city corresponds to the fixed costs that were incurred when they were erected. This scenario fits in well with the US situation, where every private entrepreneur can assemble land to build a few houses, offices and a shopping centre: central government has nothing to say about that. If a city in this situation wants to draw more inhabitants in order to profit from the scale advantages, this will not be at the expense of the scale of other cities, but of their number. Why? As long as the number of cities is not changed, the growth of this one city will lead to a fall in the demand for housing in the others. This fall in the demand for housing translates into a lower land value surplus. The creation of the marginal city is then no longer profitable, since the fixed costs can no longer be financed from this land value surplus, so, fewer new cities are created. The consequence is that, in fact, cities no longer reckon with one another. The policy of the one city has no influence on the housing needs in the other, as long as they both exist. Consequently, whatever is best for a separate city corresponds to whatever is desirable from a social point of view. If the central government does not succeed in curbing the negative external effect of the creation of new cities, it no longer needs to concern itself with the old either. Let the Moe Greens of this world go their own sweet way.

In this setting, it is beneficial for cities to 'subsidise' land by relaxing spatial planning policy. Restrictions on the use of land exist for good reason: they are a way of protecting open space, the value of which is not expressed in market prices. By relaxing their policy, the city council fritters away some of that open space, with a social price tag attached. At the same time, however, productivity rises as the scale increases. The spatial policy will have to be relaxed and relaxed until building on an additional hectare costs as much in terms of forgone open space value as it renders in productivity profit. Does this lead to the best conceivable balance? No, it does not, because a land subsidy is not a wage subsidy. It is merely a second-best instrument. By not confronting households with the full sum of social costs for the use of land, they go for plots that are too big, and the density in the cities becomes too low. There is a clear connection between land prices and plot sizes (see Figure 2.5). In this scenario, cities still do not attain an efficient scale and hence, there will be too many of them.

If so, what about the widespread idea that cities – especially in developing countries – are overpopulated? Whether it is the central government or developers that erect new cities, some coordination of this process is important. In order to bear the fixed costs of the facilities, a considerable group of people have to move house simultaneously. If it all depends on the initiative of individual households, new cities would arise far too slowly, and existing cities would be too big. In countries that lack such coordination, this can be a serious problem. The same insight was also an important motivation in the Dutch growth centre policy albeit, of course, that the fact that the creation of cities requires coordination, in itself says nothing about the optimal number of cities.

CITY AND COUNTRYSIDE

The countryside has not played a significant part in this story as yet. If the households move from here, the growth of a city does not necessarily have to be at the expense of the number or size of other cities. This is exactly what urbanisation is all about: the migration from rural areas to the city. The advantages of agglomeration are, almost by definition, non-existent in those rural areas, so if cities grow this way, no scale advantages are lost elsewhere. Is the rural dweller's decision to move efficient? No, it is not, since they take into account the wage that they will earn in the city, but not their positive contribution to the productivity of other city dwellers.

If wages cannot be subsidised, it is difficult to internalise this effect in another way. Obstructing the formation of a city seems to be a realistic second-best instrument because, in reality, the government is already intensively involved in the process. However, it is not likely that the counterpart, the discouraging of living in the countryside, will ever be applied as a policy instrument. As such, this scenario strongly resembles the case in which the number of cities adapt, but the government cannot levy taxes on the creation of a city. Individual cities each go their own way. The associated policy recommendation, therefore, is that they relax their spatial planning policy for as long as needed until building on an additional hectare costs as much in terms of open space as it renders in terms of productivity gains.

SPATIAL PLANNING POLICY IN THE RANDSTAD AREA AS A NUMERIC EXAMPLE

What does this story boil down to in an actual numeric example? Supposing the spatial planning policy in the Randstad area were to internalise precisely the value of open space, but that it was not used as an instrument to further exploit the agglomeration benefits. How should that policy be adapted in the different scenarios? To what changes in the number of cities and their sizes would that lead? How would the result relate to the situation in which a wage subsidy is available? In order to introduce the numeric example, Figure 7.2 shows seven MAs within the Randstad area, and the first two columns in Table 7.1 present their sizes in terms of the number of households and the surface area of residential land, respectively. The influence of

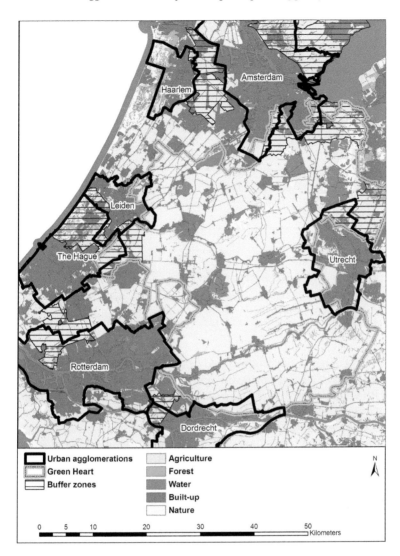

Notes:
In black: MA boundaries.

Sources: Land use in 2003 and the boundaries of the MAs were provided by CBS
Statistics Netherlands. The boundaries of the 'Green Heart' and the state-imposed buffer
zones were based on the National Spatial Strategy report (*Nota Ruimte*). The map was
created by Splinlab, VU University Amsterdam.

Figure 7.2   *City expansion is obstructed by the 'Green Heart' and the*
            state-imposed buffer zones

Table 7.1   Seven cities in the Randstad area in figures

MA	Observed quantities			Chosen quantities	
	Number of households (× 1000)	Surface area of residential land (hectares)	Shadow price of spatial planning (€/m²)	Wage level (× €1000)	Amenity level
Amsterdam	527	7964	254	24.0	1
Rotterdam	477	8553	47	24.0	0.913
The Hague	305	5355	164	23.7	0.901
Utrecht	191	3837	108	23.5	0.861
Leiden	114	2467	182	23.3	0.866
Dordrecht	102	2751	84	23.2	0.848
Haarlem	89	2205	109	23.2	0.824

Notes:
See the main text for an explanation on the way in which the wages and the level of amenities were obtained.

Sources: The number of households in 2002 and the surface area of residential land in 2003: CBS Statistics Netherlands.
The shadow price of spatial planning restrictions: RIGO Area Research and Advice.

spatial planning policy is illustrated in the figure by the boundaries in the 'Green Heart' (*Groene Hart*), the sparsely populated national park within the Randstad area, and the state-imposed buffer zones (*Rijksbufferzones*) that were allocated to separate urban areas in order to control urbanisation. There is ample land to build on in these areas, but policy dictates the preservation of the open spaces. This prevents the fusion of cities such as Amsterdam and Haarlem or Rotterdam and The Hague.

The third column in Table 7.1 shows a rough estimate of the shadow price of this kind of restriction: an indication of how binding they are. This estimate is obtained by comparing the value of residential building land on certain development sites near the edge of the city with the value of the land when it is used for alternative purposes plus the costs of preparing it for building. A great difference between these indicates that developers would like to build on far more open space in the direct vicinity than policy allows. For Amsterdam, for instance, we looked at a development site in the Bovenkerkerpolder. The shadow price here is relatively high, so that, without spatial planning policy, this city would indeed have been far larger. It is furthermore striking that land prices and, therefore, the shadow prices, at the edge of the seven cities differ widely. In Leiden and The Hague, households are also prepared to pay much more for a square metre than in Rotterdam or Dordrecht. This is a reflection of spatial planning policy that can only be rationalised with the value of open space, if that value also strongly differs from city to city. Households should, therefore, have a relatively high appreciation for the green spaces around Amsterdam, Leiden and The Hague.

The seven cities together house almost two-thirds of the total number of households in the Randstad area. Now suppose that the rest live in identical cities that all resemble Haarlem, the smallest of the MAs. The fixed costs involved in creating a city must then correspond to the surplus that is realised in the latter of these identical cities: Moe Green would no longer be able to make a profit with a new town, and neither would the government in the absence of agglomeration benefits.

Even though spatial planning policy in this imaginary experiment ignores the existence of agglomeration benefits, they are there. Chapter 4 demonstrated that productivity in a city grows by approximately 0.2 per cent if its number of households increases by 10 per cent. If the wage in Amsterdam is EUR 24000 – approximately the average disposable household income in this city – the wage in the other cities follows from this scale elasticity and the population number in the second column of Table 7.1. The outcome is included in the fourth column. The wages in the smallest city, Haarlem, would then be about EUR 800 lower. We corrected for the composition of the urban labour supply in this estimate of the wage differences.

Wages alone cannot explain why one city is so much bigger and more expensive than the other; this has something to do with the consumer amenities. The question as to which amenities matter the most has already been extensively addressed in Chapter 5. The last column in Table 7.1 shows the differences in appeal compared to Amsterdam that are needed in this numerical example to properly match the population numbers in the other cities, taking into account the differences in land prices. There are major differences at play here: if the wages in The Hague were to fall another 10 per cent vis-à-vis Amsterdam, this would have the same effect as the difference in amenities in this table.

Figure 7.3 shows the distribution of households in the different scenarios; the cities have been ordered according to their size. The point of departure is the baseline scenario that corresponds to the figures in Table 7.1. Apart from the seven MAs, this scenario includes some sixteen small cities where the rest of the Randstad population lives. In Scenario 1, this number of cities is a given, but spatial planning policy at the edge of the city has been adapted to make better use of agglomeration advantages. This is barely visible in the figure: the number of households in each city is virtually the same in both scenarios. A closer look reveals that the larger cities have grown somewhat bigger and the smaller cities have become somewhat smaller.

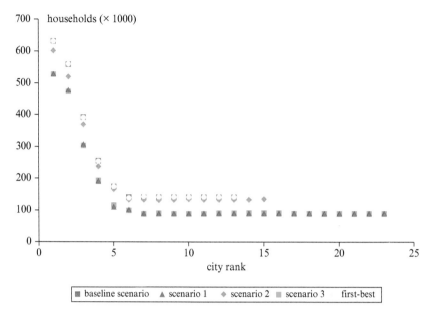

Figure 7.3   More households in fewer cities, unless the number of cities is a given

Figure 7.1, which is based on the figures for Amsterdam as the large city and Haarlem as the small city, has already illustrated the underlying mechanism: profit in the one city is partly cancelled out by the loss in the other. In this numerical example there is little variance between cities where the difference between marginal and average productivity is concerned. That is why there is little to gain from an adaptation of spatial planning policy. Table 7.2 shows the surplus in both scenarios and the profit that is earned in Scenario 1 in comparison with the baseline scenario, as contribution to the profit that would be gained in a first-best scenario. This profit indeed turns out to be negligible.

In Scenario 2, the number of cities adapts, but the government does not have the instruments to internalise the external effect that goes with it. This scenario can be interpreted as the situation in which all households live in the countryside outside the seven MAs, which shrinks when the cities grow. A relaxation of spatial planning policy is desirable in all cities in this scenario, and Figure 7.4 shows the extent to which it should relax. The horizontal axis in this figure represents the value of open space, and the vertical axis is the part of that value that should be internalised by a relaxed spatial planning policy. As Figure 7.3 shows,

Table 7.2   Adaptation of policy is somewhat profitable, unless the number of cities is a given

Scenario	Surplus (billion euro, annually)	Contribution to profit, first-best (%)
Baseline scenario	2.20	
Scenario 1: the number of cities is fixed	2.20	0.0
Scenario 2: growth at the expense of number of cities or countryside	2.39	79.6
Scenario 3: city creation is taxed	2.43	100
First-best	2.43	100

Notes:
The third column shows the percentage of the welfare gain if we change from the basic scenario to the first-best scenario, obtained in the relevant scenario.

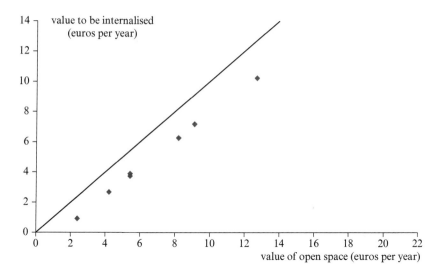

Figure 7.4   Spatial planning policy at the edge of the city must be relaxed if urban growth is at the expense of the countryside

all cities grow considerably by an average of almost 50 000 dwellings as a consequence of this relaxation. This growth is at the expense of some eight small cities, or approximately half of the countryside dwellers. The welfare gain would boil down to approximately EUR 200 million per year, or 0.25 per cent of the value of total production (see again, Table 7.2). Almost 80 per cent of the potential welfare gain from progressing from the baseline scenario to the first-best allocation would hereby already be achieved.

In Scenario 3, the tax on the creation of new cities is available. Once the optimal number of cities has been chosen, the optimal open space tax proves to be hardly different from the value of that open space. However, Figure 7.3 illustrates that the number of households per city is greater in this scenario than in Scenario 2, at the expense of another two small cities. Although policy should, therefore, not become much more, or less, restrictive in terms of the associated shadow prices, this scenario certainly asks for a substantial expansion of the housing supply in large cities. Both in terms of the resulting equilibrium and in terms of the gain in welfare of approximately EUR 230 million, or 0.3 per cent of the value of the total production that this achieves, Scenario 3 hardly differs from the first-best equilibrium. All cities get the same push by the restriction on city creation, but since they hardly vary in the difference between marginal and average production, this leads to almost the same result as a city-specific wage subsidy. The manner in which the policy should be adapted thus proves to be strongly correlated with the variation across cities in the difference between the marginal and average product of labour. In this numerical example, this variation is very limited, but so is the empirical knowledge about it so far.

THE FIVE MOST IMPORTANT CONCLUSIONS

If the number of cities and the total urban population number are fixed, the agglomeration advantage in the one city is cancelled out by the loss elsewhere.

If the total urban population number is fixed, the creation of a new city is at the expense of the productivity in existing cities. This calls for a restriction on city creation.

If the growth of the urban population is at the expense of the countryside, spatial planning policy at the edge of successful cities should be relaxed.

Within the Randstad area, the one city experiences far more restrictions from spatial planning policy than the other. This cannot be justified in itself, unless open space in the one city is more valuable than in the other.

Whether spatial planning policy reckons with external agglomeration advantages or not, can make a difference in the desired city size of around 20%.

FURTHER READING

Hesham Abdel-Rahman and Alex Anas, 2004, Theories of systems of cities, in: J. Vernon Henderson and Jacques-François Thisse (eds), *Handbook of Regional and Urban Economics, Volume 4*, 2293–2339, North-Holland/Elsevier, Amsterdam.

Annet Bleich, 2008, Joop den Uyl 1919–1987: Dromer, doordouwer, Dissertation, Amsterdam University.

J. Vernon Henderson and Hyoung Gun Wang, 2007, Urbanization and city growth: the role of institutions, *Regional Science and Urban Economics*, 37, 283–313.

Esteban Rossi-Hansberg, 2004, Optimal urban land use and zoning, *Review of Economic Dynamics*, 7, 69–106.

Wouter Vermeulen and Jos van Ommeren, 2009, Does land use planning shape regional economies? A simultaneous analysis of housing supply, internal migration and local employment growth in the Netherlands, *Journal of Housing Economics*, 18, 294–310.

8. Social cost–benefit analysis of an inner-city transformation project

> An SCBA is a valuable measurement tool, but not appropriate for urbanisation processes or metropolitan developments.
> Adri Duivesteijn, 2009

The instrument of the social cost–benefit analysis (SCBA) has been widely accepted in the assessment of investments in infrastructure, but it has led to fierce discussions in recent applications in the domain of land development. Former minister Jacqueline Cramer, for instance, stated in a parliament debate about the spending of the budget for the National Spatial Strategy that this instrument is not always equipped for the 'complexity and integrality and the long term orientation' that is required in the decision making for these kinds of projects. Adri Duivesteijn, former alderman for spatial planning in Almere, even classified the SCBA as a measurement tool unfit for urbanisation processes or metropolitan developments.

The recently published 'Guideline for SCBAs of integral area development' (*Werkwijzer MKBA van integrale gebiedsontwikkeling*) blamed the criticism partly on the differences in ways of thinking between economists and planners, and partly on the specific characteristics of integral land development. Many of the effects of, for example, landscape preservation, the creation of urban scenery or the exploitation of agglomeration benefits, are difficult to measure and evaluate. Another specific characteristic of land development is that the execution of a local project influences the investment decisions of other actors in other locations. The question arises as to with which alternative scenario the project should be compared. Finally, the local benefits could be cancelled out by costs elsewhere, such as a shift in employment, so that they do not contribute to the welfare of society as a whole.

How can the theoretical and empirical insights in this book contribute to conducting a proper SCBA of area development, supposing that a centrally located industrial estate is converted into a residential area? There are more than ample examples of obsolete industrial estates in top locations. They are the heritage of a time when raw materials and products had to be transported by train or boat. What are the relevant external effects? How great are these in comparison with the benefits within the transformed area, and on which factors does that depend? This chapter focuses on three frequently mentioned external effects of inner-city transformation projects. First, the project takes away a source of nuisance for the surroundings that stems, for instance, from smell or noise pollution. Second, the increase in the number of households in the city indirectly leads to agglomeration benefits: workers contribute to the build-up of knowledge, but are not paid for this. Third, inner-city building generates additional benefits, since it makes the development of greenfield land unnecessary and thus preserves valuable open space. All these effects have an external character, as they do not benefit the owner of the project area but rather other parties.

Again, the monocentric model of the city is our point of departure. In this chapter, however, we take into account the differences between locations, which are not equally appreciated by all households. Some are simply crazy about Rotterdam, while others are strongly attached to the countryside. If a city grows, the land must become increasingly cheaper if it wants to persuade households with a slight preference for that city to live there. Should that land price reduction for existing locations be regarded as a debit item in the balance book for the project? Or do some households benefit, since they have to pay less to the owner of their land? What does this mean for a cost–benefit analysis?

In order to make the theoretical insights a bit less abstract, we will again discuss a concrete example in this chapter. This time it is based on the SCBA of the Waal riverfront in Nijmegen, which is one of the projects partly funded by the budget for the National Spatial Strategy. The project comprises the relocation of businesses from the Waal riverfront to a location outside Nijmegen city, so that the available land can be used for the development of residential dwellings. The project area is outlined in yellow in Figure 8.1. The industrial estate causes smell, noise, and traffic pollution in an area that is outlined in white in the same figure. The unpleasant smells originate from a producer of ketchup and an abattoir, amongst others. The benefits of their removal have been estimated in the SCBA of this project at approximately 10 to 20 per cent of the benefits in the project area itself. The submitters of the grant application included the preservation of open space as a benefit, since the project would make new building in expansion locations unnecessary. Similar external effects have been claimed in most other inner-city transformation projects that were eligible for a grant from the National Spatial Strategy budget. Although the Nijmegen Waal riverfront project does not mention the utilisation of agglomeration advantages, which is the third external effect that will be discussed in this chapter, it has played a role in the SCBAs of other

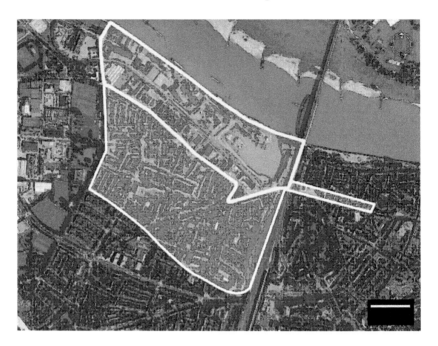

Source: Cost–benefit analysis for the Waal riverfront in Nijmegen by Buck Consultants International.

Figure 8.1   The project area by the Waal River and the contours of the pollution

projects funded from the same budget, such as the Rotterdam City Port project.

THE WELFARE EFFECTS OF THE TRANSFORMATION PROJECT

What does the owner of a centrally located industrial estate stand to gain from transforming it into a residential area? He rakes in the land value of the new residential dwellings. These are the benefits that the land owner internalises. What are the costs in exchange? If the businesses close down, the value of the land in its old function counts as a debit item. When they are relocated to a location outside the city, the removal cost should be taken into account, as well as the costs of the new piece of land, including the value of any open space that is lost. The clean-up and preparation of the soil for building can also be a very expensive affair. Does the landowner, who maximises their profit, make an efficient decision? That depends on the external effects.

Suppose that the industrial estate is a source of nuisance for the surrounding residents. In a spatial equilibrium, these households are just as well off as elsewhere, otherwise they would have moved. The negative value of the nuisance is thus reflected in the land prices around the industrial estate. Henri de Groot and Friso de Vor have performed this exercise for the Randstad area and the Noord-Brabant province. Jan Rouwendal and Willemijn van der Straaten made an estimate of the negative impact of industrial estates on the prices of nearby residential dwellings in Amsterdam, Rotterdam, and The Hague. Both studies are used here. The transformation project makes the source of nuisance disappear, so land prices rise. The beneficiaries of this are the landowners near the industrial estate.

For the same reason, the agglomeration advantages are reflected in land prices. Due to the transformation project, the number of inhabitants of the city rises, and so does the number of jobs. The empirical results of Chapter 4 can be used to gauge the effect of this rise in urban density and scale on wages. The land price will have to continue to rise until the households no longer care as to whether they live in this city or elsewhere. Eventually, therefore, it is the landowners in the rest of the city that profit from these two external effects. Consumers will be none the wiser, unless they own land. Whatever they gain from the reduction in inconvenience or higher wages due to the increase in economic density, they lose to a rise in land prices.

How does this story run if households differ in their preference for the city of Nijmegen? The demand for residential dwellings in Nijmegen depends on how badly people would like to live there in comparison with other places in the country. It is the people with the strongest attachment to Nijmegen who will actually go and live there. As the city grows, for instance after new building in the former industrial estate, it will draw households with an increasingly more limited attachment. Land prices will have to fall if new residents are to be persuaded to buy a house in the city. Now it is not the land owners who benefit, but rather the households that are already living in the city. Their living there has become cheaper, thanks to the transformation project. Home owners also profit in this respect, but they are making a loss on the land underneath their homes at the same time. All in all they are equally well off: there is a transfer from land owners to consumers, but no additional welfare effect.

Figure 8.2 shows land prices, both before and after the transformation of an industrial estate, as a function of the distance to the city centre. It

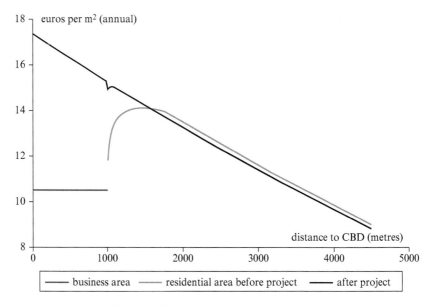

Figure 8.2   The change in land value captures part of the benefits

is based on the numerical example that will be discussed in the next paragraph. The internal benefits equal the value of the transformed land, and the figure also illustrates its value in its old function. Around the industrial estate, land prices rise, due to the removal of the nuisance. At a greater distance, however, they fall. Hence, in this example, the downward effect that is due to the differences in preferences is greater than the positive effect of the agglomeration benefits. This change in land prices does not, however, equal the total benefits from the project, since a transfer to consumers is also incorporated.

This is not yet the whole story. What if it concerns the transformation of a major industrial estate, so that a considerable number of new households may be welcomed to the city? Land prices must fall until the very last household among these newcomers, which feels the least attachment to Nijmegen, is indifferent. What about the other newcomers? These are better off than before the project, just like the households that already lived in the city. They would have been prepared to move to Nijmegen and pay a higher price for their land, but due to that marginal household they could keep part of their money in their pockets. This newcomer surplus is not cancelled out by the land price fall in the existing city – which was cancelled out by the surplus of the households that already lived there – so this is an additional welfare effect.

NIJMEGEN WAAL RIVERFRONT PROJECT AS A NUMERICAL EXAMPLE

What is the importance of all these effects in comparison with the internal benefits? And on what factors does the magnitude of these effects depend? A concrete example may clarify this. Let us regard Nijmegen as a mono-centric city. There is an industrial estate that ranges from the CBD to one kilometre outside it. Houses cannot be built everywhere, so we end up with a residential neighbourhood of approximately 100 hectares, which makes the radius larger than the Waal riverfront project actually is. The number of homes – 80 000 before the start of the project – increases by 6 per cent. The distribution of preferences for living in this city is determined as such, so that the number of households that wish to live in Nijmegen increases by 2 per cent if the land price for an average spot in the city falls by 1 per cent. The marginal household must, therefore, be rather sensitive to land prices, which seems to be reasonable since there are sufficient other housing locations around Nijmegen.

The industrial estate causes the surrounding households inconvenience. The effect of that inconvenience on the house prices has been empirically extensively researched. In the first variant discussed below, the influence of the nuisance from the industrial estate corresponds to the results of the estimate by Friso de Vor and Henri de Groot for the Noord-Brabant province (see further reading). According to them, this influence ranges up to 750 metres from the industrial estate. The second variant is based on the study by Jan Rouwendal and Willemijn van der Straaten for Rotterdam (see further reading). In their study, the influence of the industrial estate reaches less far, namely up to 500 metres. The agglomeration effect has the same magnitude as in the previous chapter. If the employment adapts and also rises by 6 per cent, the wages will slightly increase by 0.1 per cent.

Table 8.1 shows the benefits of an urban transformation project for the industrial estate described. For the purpose of comparison, two other projects have also been included, for a smaller and a larger area. All items are expressed in EUR millions per year. The costs of the project have been omitted, since only the relative importance of the external benefits is of concern here. The internal benefits of the basic projects amount to almost EUR 17 million per year; with a discount rate of 5.5 per cent, this equals a cash value of around EUR 300 million. Based on the estimates made by Friso de Vor and Henri de Groot, the removal of nuisance renders an external effect at the value of 10 per cent of the direct benefits, and the indirect agglomeration benefits run up to more than 15 per cent. The newcomer surplus appears to be negligible: a little more than 1 per cent.

Table 8.1   In a greater project, the relative importance of nuisance
decreases, but the newcomer surplus and the transfers become
more important

	Small project	Basic project	Major project
	(25 hectares)	(100 hectares)	(400 hectares)
Internal benefits	4.30	16.54	61.73
Removal of nuisance	0.98	1.59	2.67
Agglomeration effect	0.63	2.43	8.80
Newcomer surplus	0.01	0.19	2.23
Transfer	1.72	6.37	20.06

Notes:
All items are expressed in EUR millions per year. Nuisance is based on Friso de Vor and
Henri de Groot.

However, there is a relatively considerable transfer from landowners to
consumers.

How do these effects change for bigger projects? If the surface of the
transformed area doubles, the internal benefits and agglomeration benefits double. However, the relative importance of the removal of nuisance
decreases: in the major project this benefit amounts to less than 5 per cent
of the direct benefits. The reason for this is that this external effect only
occurs at the edge of the project area. The effect of the removal of nuisance within the area itself is reflected in the price of the transformed land;
this latter effect is comparably more important in larger projects. The
newcomer surplus, on the other hand, increases more than proportionally: for the major project, this benefit is even comparable in magnitude
to the removal of the nuisance. This is due to the fact that the marginal
newcomer's attachment to the city will increasingly differ from the preferences of the present residents. It must be noted though, that the major
project, in which the residential surface area in Nijmegen would rise by
approximately 20 per cent, is considerably larger than the inner-city transformation projects that were eligible for a grant from the National Spatial
Strategy budget.

How do the benefits of the project correlate with the extent to which
the preferences of households differ? The greater these differences, the
less elastic the demand for homes in the city. New households will, after
all, have to be offered a higher discount if they are to cross the threshold.
In Table 8.2, the magnitude of the project remains constant, but the price
elasticity of the demand for plots in the city varies. With an elasticity of

Table 8.2   Newcomer surplus and transfer are less important when the housing demand is more elastic

	Demand elasticity of −1	Demand elasticity of −2 (basic)	Demand elasticity of minus infinity
Internal benefits	16.16	16.54	16.95
Removal of nuisance	1.86	1.86	1.86
Agglomeration effect	2.40	2.43	2.47
Newcomer surplus	0.38	0.19	0
Transfer	12.53	6.36	0

Notes:
All items are expressed in EUR millions per year. Nuisance is based on the estimates for Rotterdam by Jan Rouwendal and Willemijn van der Straaten.

−1, when the attachment to the city plays a greater role, the newcomer surplus and the transfer are greater. With an elasticity of minus infinity, when everyone is the same and the attachment to the city plays no role, there is in fact no newcomer surplus and transfer. The internal benefits of the project are smaller when the demand is less elastic. If we compare the first column in the table with the third, we see that its decline is about twice as big as the rise in the newcomer surplus. The middle column of Table 8.2 is in all other respects comparable with the middle column in Table 8.1. The external effect of the removal of the nuisance is just a bit greater. The results are, therefore, solid in this respect.

Naturally, the external effects also depend on the importance of agglomeration advantages. Table 8.3 illustrates the extent to which this is indeed the case. The external agglomeration benefits increase in proportion to the scale elasticity. There is also a limited effect on the internal benefits: the value of the land in the project areas also increases if there are agglomeration effects that are greater. All other items remain virtually the same.

DOES AN INNER CITY PROJECT PRESERVE VALUABLE OPEN SPACE?

Land development is a long-term process that takes place with a view to future housing demand. This may mean that inner-city transformation projects must be weighed against alternative development projects, such as building at greenfield locations at the edge of the city. Is such an exchange important in an SCBA? It is not, when the benefits of the project are weighed against the current situation; after all, the project does not create

Table 8.3   Agglomeration benefits increase in proportion to the scale elasticity

	Scale elasticity of 0	Scale elasticity of 0.01	Scale elasticity of 0.03
Internal benefits	16.39	16.46	16.61
Removal of nuisance	1.59	1.59	1.59
Agglomeration effect	0	1.21	3.66
Newcomer surplus	0.19	0.19	0.20
Transfer	6.34	6.35	6.38

Notes:
All items are expressed in EUR millions per year. Nuisance is based on estimates for the Noord-Brabant province by Friso de Vor and Henri de Groot.

open space. Worse still, if it concerns the relocation of business to an area outside the city, it even means that open space is being sacrificed. If the project is not executed, however, it might be advantageous to build houses at the edge of the city. Compared to this alternative project, the inner-city transformation does preserve open space.

How much open space is being preserved in comparison with an alternative at the edge of the city which, in terms of spatial planning policy, is equally restrictive? At what point does this generate an additional welfare effect? In order to be able to answer these questions, it is useful to interpret the boundaries of the city as an equilibrium outcome in the land market. In reality, the zoning plan determines where urban building stops, but the same outcome could be reached by taxing the conversion of open space. Land will then be developed when the price of that land exceeds the costs of preparing it for building, the value of agricultural land and this open space tax. The project does not affect the value of open space, so the tax also remains the same. This way, the restrictiveness of the spatial planning policy is maintained at a constant level.

In a reference alternative where the inner-city transformation project is not executed, the edge of the city will shift further outward at the expense of open space, provided that the households' preferences for living in the city sufficiently diverge. The difference between the value of the land at the edge of the city, which is being preserved by the transformation project, and the value that it would have after building constitutes a welfare effect that is additional to the costs and benefits discussed before. The magnitude of this difference strongly depends on the degree to which the value of open space is already being internalised by the spatial planning policy at the edge of the city. Suppose that the open space tax equals the value of open space. In that case, the value of the preserved land as open space corresponds to the value that this land would have after building. The additional welfare effect is, therefore, negligible.

The previous chapter showed that it may be a good idea to relax spatial planning policy relative to the value of open space in order to further exploit agglomeration benefits. The open space tax could also be less than this value if the government does not have sufficient instruments to internalise it; property rights, for instance, could be an obstruction. However, the question remains to what extent this is an issue in the Dutch context, since new building always requires the approval of a local government in the Netherlands. Naturally, there is also the possibility that spatial planning policy is too restrictive.

How much open space is being preserved in comparison with the reference alternative and what this renders in terms of prosperity is not only dependent on the spatial planning policy at the edge of the city, but also on the demand and scale elasticities. Table 8.4 illustrates the influence of these three factors. In the upper section, the role of agglomeration advantages has been taken to be non-existent. The demand elasticity varies over the columns in the same way as in Table 8.3. The different rows show the magnitude of the welfare effect in EUR millions per year if the open space tax equals the value of open space, or if the spatial planning policy is less restrictive. With a demand elasticity of −2 and in the absence of scale

Table 8.4   Preservation of open space hardly generates additional benefits, unless the spatial planning policy at the edge of the city fails

	Demand elasticity of −1	Demand elasticity of −2 (basic)	Demand elasticity of minus infinity
No scale advantages in production			
Value of open space = tax	0.15	0.07	0
Value = tax + 1 €/m²	0.85	0.54	0
Value = tax + 2 €/m²	1.55	1.02	0
Value = tax + 5 €/m²	3.64	2.44	0
Scale elasticity of 0.02 as in the basic scenario			
Value of open space = tax	0.12	0.03	0.12
Value = tax + 1 €/m²	0.73	0.33	−1.08
Value = tax + 2 €/m²	1.34	0.63	−2.28
Value = tax + 5 €/m²	3.16	1.52	−5.88

Notes:
All items are expressed in EUR millions per year. Nuisance is based on estimates for the Noord-Brabant province by Friso de Vor and Henri de Groot.

advantages, the transformation of an industrial estate of 100 hectares preserves about 50 hectares of greenfield land. When the spatial planning policy at the edge of the city internalises the value of this open space, the net effect on prosperity turns out to be indeed more or less negligible: for a project of a marginal magnitude it precisely equals 0. However, there may be substantial benefit involved, if the open space tax is lower. If the annual value of open space exceeds the open space tax by EUR 5 per square metre, this effect runs up to 15 per cent of the internal benefits.

The amount of preserved open space is larger when the demand for homes in the city is less sensitive to prices. In case of infinite demand elasticity, new construction in the centre has no influence on the demand for land at the edge of the city as long as agglomeration benefits do not play a role. This means that for a project of non-marginal magnitude there are also no additional benefits, even if the difference between the open space tax and the value of open space is substantial. When the demand is less elastic, the benefits are actually greater. The scenario where the demand elasticity equals −1 preserves 70 hectares of open space.

If agglomeration economies were to play a role, as in the bottom section of Table 8.4, new construction on greenfield land would generate additional agglomeration benefits. The preservation of open space at the edge of this city is less attractive in this case, for we also lose a bit of scale at the same time. In the first two columns, the benefits in the bottom section are, therefore, smaller than in the upper section. Moreover, the indirect agglomeration benefit in the rest of the city is smaller, since there is a smaller addition of households than in the reference alternative. However, in the third column, with infinite demand elasticity, something remarkable happens. The housing demand at the edge of the city grows greater rather than smaller when the transformation project is executed. After all, the project leads to higher wages, thus drawing more people to the city: in this scenario, new households do not have less fondness for the city than the people who already live there. The consequence is that 120 hectares more open space is being sacrificed in the expansion locations than in the reference scenario. This does not matter so much if the tax on open space equals its value, but it may lead to substantial additional costs if it is lower. These are counteracted by the positive agglomeration benefits in the rest of the city. Those make it attractive to pursue a more relaxed spatial planning policy than the direct benefits alone would justify.

THE FIVE MOST IMPORTANT CONCLUSIONS

An SCBA is a good instrument for mapping out the external effects of area development.

External effects of nuisance and scale advantages can substantially raise the total benefits of a project, but the major part is absorbed by the project area itself.

The preservation of open space generates hardly any additional welfare gains if its value has already been taken into account in the spatial planning policy at the edge of the city.

If the house prices in a city fall due to additional supply, the welfare effects of a transformation project will not be fully reflected in the land prices. This effect, however, is negligible for projects of a normal magnitude.

The decline in house prices may, however, lead to a substantial transfer from land owners to residents.

FURTHER READING

Centraal Planbureau and Planbureau voor de Leefomgeving, *Evaluatie beoordelingen Nota Ruimteprojecten*, The Hague, 20 September 2010.

Denise DiPasquale and William Wheaton, 1996, *Urban Economics and Real Estate Markets*, Prentice Hall, New Jersey.

Ecorys i.c.w. and Witteveen + Bos, 2009, *Werkwijzer MKBA van integrale gebiedsontwikkeling*, Rotterdam.

Jan Rouwendal and Willemijn van der Straaten, 2008, The costs and benefits of providing open space in cities, Tinbergen Institute Discussion Paper 2008-001/3, Amsterdam-Rotterdam.

Friso de Vor and Henri de Groot, 2011, The impact of industrial sites on residential property values: a hedonic pricing analysis from the Netherlands, *Regional Studies*, 45(5), 609–23.

9. Agenda for the future

Prices are determined by three factors: location, location and location.
Old real estate brokers' maxim

This old maxim is the shortest summary imaginable for this book. Location is the one and all-deciding determinant of the price of real estate. In many parts of the Dutch countryside, a square metre of land for residential purposes yields less than EUR 20; for the most attractive bits of land in Amsterdam and The Hague, the price is a factor of 200 higher. That price difference between 'city' and 'countryside' has more than doubled in the past 20 years. The prices in the north wing of the Randstad area, around the Brabant city triangle of Breda–'s-Hertogenbosch–Eindhoven, and in the inner city of Maastricht have risen twice as fast during those years as the prices in Zeeuws-Vlaanderen or the rural areas of the provinces of Groningen and Drenthe. The importance of location has only grown. It has turned out that these differences in value can be explained. The accessibility, by car or public transport, the wage level in the surroundings, the availability of amenities such as shops, bars and performing arts, the presence of a seventeenth-century city centre, or attractive natural amenities – all these factors are highly relevant to the price of a plot of land.

LAND VALUE SURPLUS, CITIES AND LOCAL PUBLIC FACILITIES

The great importance of the clustering of economic activities has far-reaching consequences for economic policy. The sensitivity of the land price to its surroundings by definition means that important external effects occur. The investment in a property by a single owner increases the value of the adjacent plots. Owners, however, do not include this positive external effect on their neighbours' property in their decision to invest and, therefore, they invest less than would be desirable from a social point of view. So the market fails. There is a market for governmental intervention and spatial planning to repair this market failure.

The backdrop of these external effects is scale advantages. Public facilities in the widest sense of the word need great support in order to spread the fixed costs of such facilities over sufficiently wide target groups. Since there is not sufficient potential or support to realise these facilities at every location, the land in their vicinity is more valuable. More than that, the Henry George Theorem (HGT) states that in equilibrium, the land value surplus in the surroundings of a public facility equals the costs of that facility, and according to Paul Samuelson's Rule (PSR), a public administrator who tries to maximise the land value surplus by realising an adequate package of public facilities, maximises social prosperity at the same time.

From the standpoint of economic theory, therefore, this land-value-maximising public administrator fulfils the same role as the profit-hunting entrepreneur: both improve the effective design of society by chasing after their own interests. Since the land value surplus is a good measure for the social return of a facility, land prices are essential building blocks for Social Cost–Benefit Analyses (SCBAs). Chapter 5 indeed demonstrates that land price differences are empirically easily explainable. The total land value surplus in the Netherlands, of land for residential purposes, amounts to EUR 340 billion, which corresponds to an annual return of approximately EUR 15 billion, or 3 per cent of GDP. The analysis in this book thus provides insight into a number of crucial parameters for policy analysis.

These parameters are, incidentally, based on an analysis of data that are not publicly available as yet. Given their importance to policy analysis, this kind of information should be publicly available for expert assessments and counterchecks. Other sources of information about land prices should also be publicly accessible for research and policy analysis. The central government should in fact have permanent data about the actual land value and the underlying causes of variance and dynamics readily available, and also for public debate. Through the land registry and information that can be deduced from stamp duty, they hold the most crucial information. The disclosure of that information is a public good.

CO-LOCATION OF FACILITIES AND DISTRIBUTIVE JUSTICE

The insight that the presence, or absence, of public facilities in the widest sense of the word is the driving force behind land price differences is directly related to the economic theory of the city. Cities are places with a vast array of public facilities, par excellence. That is why the land prices there are high, and this applies even more to the city centre, where all those facilities are within reach. Locally, the high land prices in the city centre lead to a high population density and relatively small plots. This is efficient, for as many people as possible can benefit from the proximity of public facilities that way, and the support for these facilities will be as great as possible at the same time. It is also efficient if people who do not appreciate those facilities and are not prepared to pay a high rent for half of a floor at the back of a building go and live elsewhere. Then, after all, the scarce small pieces of land in the vicinity of those facilities remain available to those who do appreciate them.

That is at odds with the dogma of the mixed neighbourhood, dominant in the Netherlands. The economic theory of the city provides good reasons to take that dogma with a pinch of salt. The ideal of the mixed neighbourhood which, it can be argued, enhances social cohesion (see the work by David Cutler and Edward Glaeser in further reading) is at loggerheads with the advantages of specialisation in the selection of facilities.

The economic theory of the city predicts that cities are concentrations of public facilities in different domains. After all, the high population density in the city provides support for numerous widely varying facilities at the same time. Success breeds success, and one facility creates the conditions for the next. This is precisely what scale advantages encompass: whatever is big becomes bigger. Distributive justice in spatial planning turns out to be a matter of grasp all, lose all. It splinters the support for good facilities, and thereby the possibility of realising them. It is not without good reason that the spatial allocation policy of government departments proved to be a disaster. Not all facilities need to be available in all cities: not every city needs its own container port. Facilities that go together logically should, as much as possible, be brought together in one location. A properly functioning city and a properly functioning system of cities are like a Swiss watch: when you take out just one of the cogwheels, the rest stops working.

One type of concentration occurs in all successful cities. Public facilities on the production side of the economy – a CBD with successful companies that is open to commuter traffic through a good network of motorways and public transport – go hand in hand with public facilities on the consumer side – luxury shops, bars and restaurants, architectural beauty and an array of cultural amenities. This nexus is understandable. If people have easy access to work in the city centre, they also have easy access to recreation there. The striking conclusion of the empirical analyses in Chapters 4 and 5 in this book is that the consumer side is at least as important to the land value surplus as the production side. This corresponds to the role of the city in the knowledge economy. Of all things, it is the innovative activities that benefit most from an urban environment. Experience teaches that innovation in the wide sense of the word best flourishes in an environment with many direct, often coincidental, contacts. The urban environment is, therefore, primarily advantageous to higher-educated people, for it is this group in particular that seeks an interesting array of cultural amenities and bars and restaurants. The degree to which a city manages to excel in its consumptive nature is, thus, the decisive factor for success on the production side. At the same time, the facilities on the consumer side are far more locally oriented than on the production side. People are prepared to travel much further for their work than for their relaxation, as shown in Chapter 5.

Although land prices are a natural point of reference for SCBAs, the occurrence of scale advantages does require special attention when it comes to facilities. What causes the high land price near the railway station – the station itself, or the many offices and residential dwellings in its direct vicinity? The one cannot do without the other, and the same applies the other way around. The value of a railway station depends on the nearby facilities and vice versa. The notions of cause and effect lose their meaning in this context: the famous chicken-and-egg problem occurs. A new railway station near an industrial estate does not only enhance the attractiveness of that estate for existing businesses, but it also makes the estate more appealing to new businesses. Conversely, there is little value in that station if the facilities nearby do not suffice. To make it even more complicated: a railway station in a residential neighbourhood only has added value if it has a direct connection with another station in a CBD that offers many jobs. The interaction of facilities, therefore, plays a major role in their impact on land value. That makes it difficult to properly distinguish the effects of individual facilities, which is needed for SCBAs. This problem can be solved, as Ioulia Ossokina (see further reading) has done, by looking into the added value of railway stations for land prices on a very detailed spatial scale, or by studying the changes in land prices whenever a new station is built somewhere. An SCBA always requires a closer analysis of the interaction between facilities.

This phenomenon of concentration of facilities in a single location always allows for multiple spatial equilibria. Once the dynamics in a certain location get going, they enhance themselves. As for the reason why location A rather than B was chosen for all those facilities, partly remains an open question. Why has Amsterdam thrived since 1985, whereas Rotterdam has not? There will always be a rational explanation for this in hindsight, but beforehand it is largely a matter of chance. Small causes can have great effects later, like the famous fluttering of a butterfly in the Amazon Delta leading to a hurricane thousands of miles away. Without the entrepreneurial spirit of Anton and Frits Philips, Eindhoven would not have been the fifth largest city in the Netherlands right now.

LAND VALUE AND PUBLIC ADMINISTRATION

The concentration of facilities in the city centre and their great external effects on the land value in the surroundings turn that city into a natural administrative unit. The subsidiarity principle dictates that the boundaries of the city region coincide with the range of the effects of the amenities in the city centre on land prices. A council for a smaller area does not internalise all the relevant external effects, whereas a government for a larger area only leads to unnecessary internal conflicts of interests and thereby to a lack of strength and variation. From this point of view many cities are just a size too small, and there is actually no legitimacy for the continued existence of most provinces in their current format.

Although the market fails and government intervention can, therefore, lead to a better result than the anarchy of the market process, designing appropriate government is not easy. In theory, a new city can be designed at the drawing table, as happened in the Netherlands where the cities of Almere, Lelystad and Zoetermeer were concerned, which were all created in the twentieth century. Spatial planning policy may demand that location A will be the hot spot where everything will happen, but it is eventually the market parties that must have faith that the government can in fact fulfil that ambition. The government has deep pockets, but the subtle cogwheels of a city do not allow themselves to be designed at the drawing board. A city grows organically while experimenting with new formats and activities. Take Amsterdam, for example. That city made its mark as a seaport city. Its ring of canals was the centre of the world for a whole century. That concentration of people made Amsterdam an ideal location for new facilities and activities in their turn, for the financial industry, the Concertgebouw and – more recently – the Internet junction. The old core activity, the port, has since turned into a bottomless pit. The economic hustle and bustle within the ring of canals has also long gone. It is only bars, restaurants, and luxury shops that remain, making the city centre a very attractive living environment. Cities continually transform themselves. Zipf's Law demonstrates that the one city is far more successful in doing so than the other. City growth is a matter of ongoing experimenting. Some experiments are a success but, inevitably, others fail. Good economic policy cannot prevent such failures, but it can make the conditions for success as advantageous as possible by internalising the external effects of public facilities as best as possible and thus create the best possible conditions for growth.

SPATIAL PLANNING POLICY AND THE OPTION VALUE OF LAND

In the land market, the uncertainty about the future development of the city is expressed in the option value of the agricultural land within its radius and other unused land, such as an obsolete industrial estate at its centre. The user value of that land in its current function may be limited but, after conversion, great fortune awaits. It may be asked why, despite the good prospects, these building plans have remained shelved up until now. There might be various reasons. First, the government may have all sorts of reasons to prevent building: zoning plans are excellent instruments for doing this. Second, the owner of the land itself might want to delay the building plans: on the one hand, this delay will cost money as there will be no rental income for the object that is to be built, but on the other it will eventually bring in money. Once a project is realised, it can only be adapted to changes in circumstances against high costs. New information about the development of the city will become available in the course of time. These new insights will allow the owner to have the building plans respond better to the current demand in the urban property market. Delay offers the owner the flexibility to adapt the plans to future needs. This is a typical example of investment under uncertainty in which irreversibility leads to delay. Be that as it may, with or without buildings, the prospects of a piece of land translate into an option value in the land price. This renders it difficult to empirically determine the precise effect of facilities on land prices, as they include facilities that have not been realised as yet. The option component in the land value, therefore, leads to numerous, both empirical and theoretical, complications in applying HGT and PSR, which need closer examination.

It should also be noted that this book only analysed the land prices of plots with a residential purpose. The next step would be the analysis of the prices of commercial properties and agricultural land. In a free land market, arbitrage takes place on the margin between land used for different purposes. If there are no external effects, this leads to efficient land use. Zoning plans limit the possibility of arbitrage. As said, there can be good reasons for doing so. An empirical analysis provides more insight into the rationality of those differences, which helps in rationalising spatial planning policy.

The inevitable implication of the coincidence of the development of cities is that there are both growing and shrinking cities. Edward Glaeser and Joseph Gyourko (see further reading) showed that growing and shrinking cities are completely different. In growing cities the housing supply adapts by new building, especially at the edge of the city, and the price rises in centres. The wage level rises as a contributory factor in the growth as well as due to that growth, since the costs of living increase further. In the case of decline, it is not obvious which houses should be demolished immediately. Demolition is, after all, money down the drain. The decline is only absorbed by falling prices in the house market. The price of buildings is normally equal to the building costs. In a shrinking city, however, the price of the buildings drops below the building costs. The price difference between plots with or without buildings is smaller than the building costs. If the building is destroyed, for instance by fire, the owner would not rebuild. Thus, the city will become cheaper than the surrounding countryside, and the wage level will also be lower than in the surrounding areas. Dutch examples are cities such as Enschede, Heerlen and Geleen/Sittard. If the city was not already there, no public administrator would ever have created it. At the same time, those low house prices offer a chance to compete on price. That too is a viable market segment.

COMPETITION BETWEEN CITIES

Since success breeds success, and because the number of leading positions is by definition limited, cities are continually in fierce competition with one another. Not every city can have a high-tech campus. The success of the one city, therefore, is at the expense of the other. However, that competition does not only take place within a fixed space. Cities differentiate: they choose their own niche, thereby creating a palette of locations that meet the wide-ranging needs of both consumers and producers. This process raises two questions. First, does free competition between cities not lead to a fruitless contest for the scarce leading positions and so to a waste of open space? Second, does the competition lead to the socially desired level of differentiation in urban living environments? As for the first question, in a simple theoretical model, competition between cities renders a reasonable result without excessive new expansions, just like monopolistic competition between businesses does not lead to enormous overcapacity. As for the second question, competition between cities results in too limited a differentiation in living environments, particularly at the upper side of the division. Supposing that two ice-cream vendors both want to set up business on a four-kilometre long beach: from a social point of view, it would be ideal if they set up their businesses at kilometre markers one and three, since beachgoers would not then have to walk more than one kilometre in either direction. However, their mutual competition urges both to place their wagon at kilometre marker two. Where differentiation between municipalities is concerned, the same applies as for differentiation within

---

THE FIVE MOST IMPORTANT CONCLUSIONS

Land price differences between and within cities and between a city and its countryside, are a sign of external effects and are, therefore, a reason for government policy.

The government of an urban agglomeration that tries to maximise the land value surplus will realise a package of public facilities that is optimal from a social point of view.

Since land price differences reflect the user benefit of local public amenities, they are an excellent basis for social cost–benefit analyses and the best tax base for financing lower governments.

Co-location of facilities makes maximum use of the advantages of urban density. Therefore, distributive justice leads to a less efficient array of facilities.

According to the subsidiarity principle, the boundaries of an urban region should coincide with the range of the effects of the centre's amenities on land prices.

---

the municipal boundaries: the dogma of the mixed municipality deserves as many pinches of salt as that of the mixed neighbourhood.

FURTHER READING

David Cutler and Edward Glaeser, 1997, Are ghettos good or bad? *Quarterly Journal of Economics*, 114(3), 827–72.

Edward Glaeser and Joseph Gyourko, 2005, Urban decline and durable housing, *Journal of Political Economy*, 113(2), 345–75.

Edward Glaeser, Matthew Kahn and Jordan Rappaport, 2008, Why do the poor live in cities? The role of public transportation, *Journal of Urban Economics*, 63(1), 1–24.

Ioulia Ossokina, 2010, Geographical range of amenity benefits: hedonic price analysis for railway stations, CPB Discussion Paper 146, The Hague.

Bas ter Weel, Albert van der Horst and George Gelauff, 2010, *The Netherlands of 2040*, Centraal Planbureau, The Hague.

Index